BRODY'S GHOST™

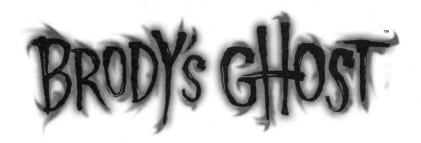

BRODY'S GHOST ™

BOOK 3

STORY AND ART BY
MARK CRILLEY

DARK HORSE BOOKS

Publisher - Mike Richardson
Designer - Kat Larson
Assistant Editor - Jemiah Jefferson
Editor - Rachel Edidin

Published by Dark Horse Books
A division of Dark Horse Comics, Inc.
10956 SE Main Street
Milwaukie, OR 97222

DarkHorse.com

To find a comic shop in your area call the Comic Shop Locator Service toll-free at (888) 266-4226

First edition: April 2012
ISBN 978-1-59582-862-0

BRODY'S GHOST BOOK 3

10 9 8 7 6 5 4 3 2 1
Printed at Lake Book Manufacturing, Inc., Melrose Park, IL, USA

THIS BOOK IS DEDICATED TO DAVE LAND,
WHO WENT TO BAT FOR THIS SERIES NOT ONCE BUT TWICE,
AND WHO TAUGHT ME TO STEER CLEAR
OF THE DREADED EXPLAINO.

THE STORY SO FAR...

Brody is a young man living in a decaying metropolis a number of decades from now. After being dumped by his girlfriend Nicole, he allowed his life to spiral into a directionless mess. One afternoon he finds himself face to face with a teenaged female ghost, Talia, who tells him she died five years earlier from leukemia, and that she won't be allowed into heaven until she unmasks a dangerous killer known as the Penny Murderer. Reluctantly, Brody offers his help. Talia leads Brody to the dwelling of the ghost of an ancient samurai, Kagemura, who takes it upon himself to train Brody in body and mind in order to gain the strength and ability to make use of Brody's latent psychic talents.

Having gained exceptional physical condition and control of his telekinetic abilities, Brody launches into a campaign of bringing down some of the city's most lethal criminals. Emboldened by his successes, Brody attempts to patch things up with Nicole just long enough to say goodbye—but as they enjoy a peaceful final afternoon together, Brody is struck by a vision of Nicole lying dead, with a penny on her forehead . . .

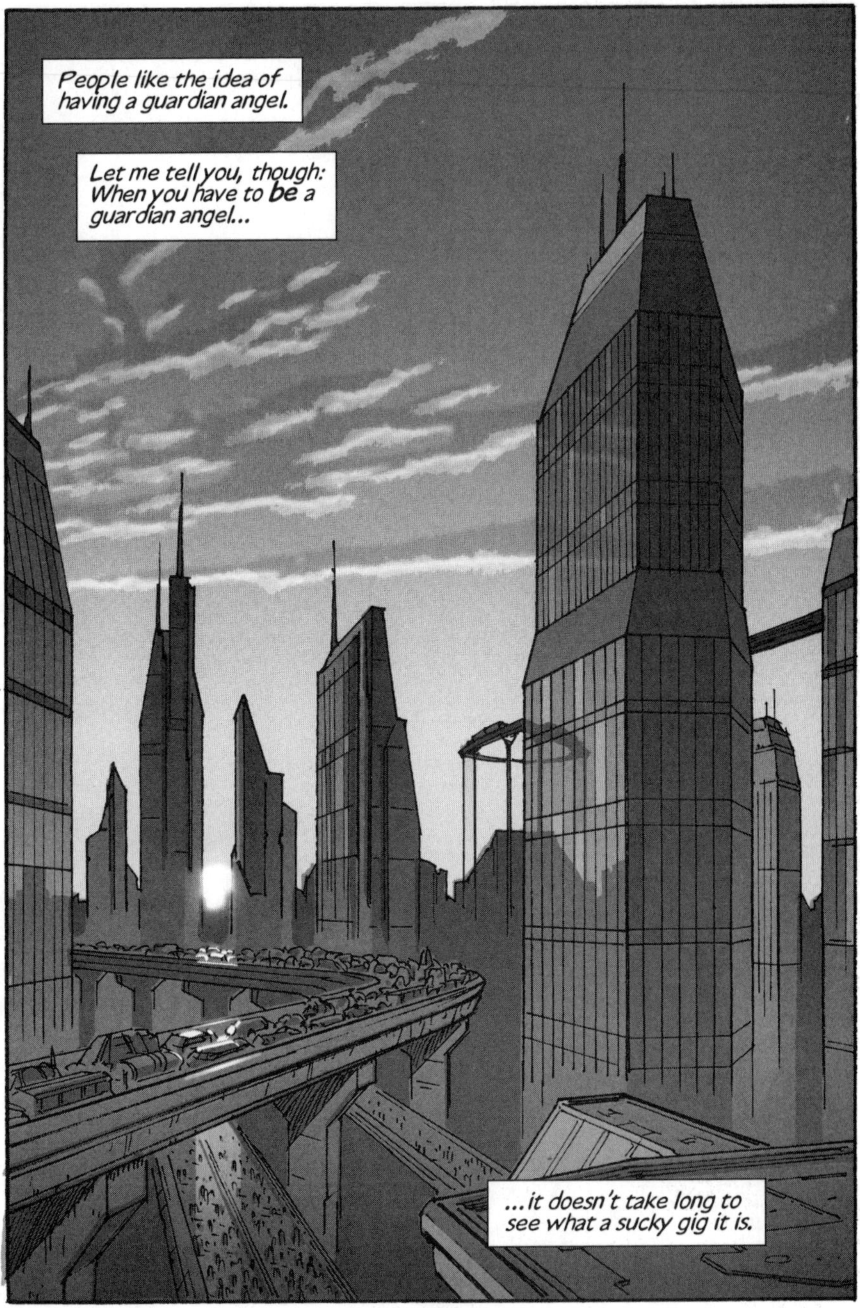
People like the idea of having a guardian angel.
Let me tell you, though: When you have to be a guardian angel...
...it doesn't take long to see what a sucky gig it is.

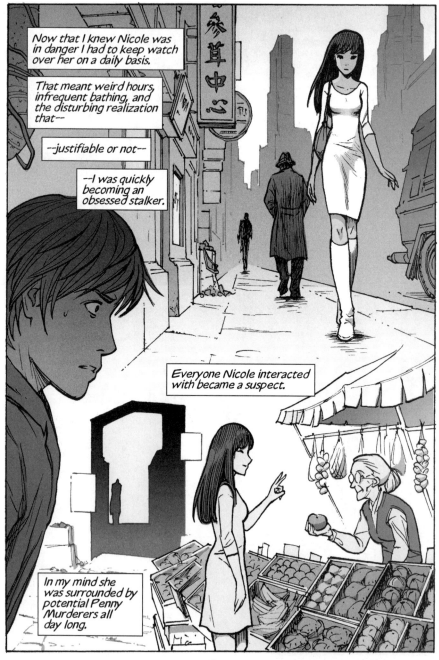

Now that I knew Nicole was in danger I had to keep watch over her on a daily basis.

That meant weird hours, infrequent bathing, and the disturbing realization that--

--justifiable or not--

--I was quickly becoming an obsessed stalker.

Everyone Nicole interacted with became a suspect.

In my mind she was surrounded by potential Penny Murderers all day long.

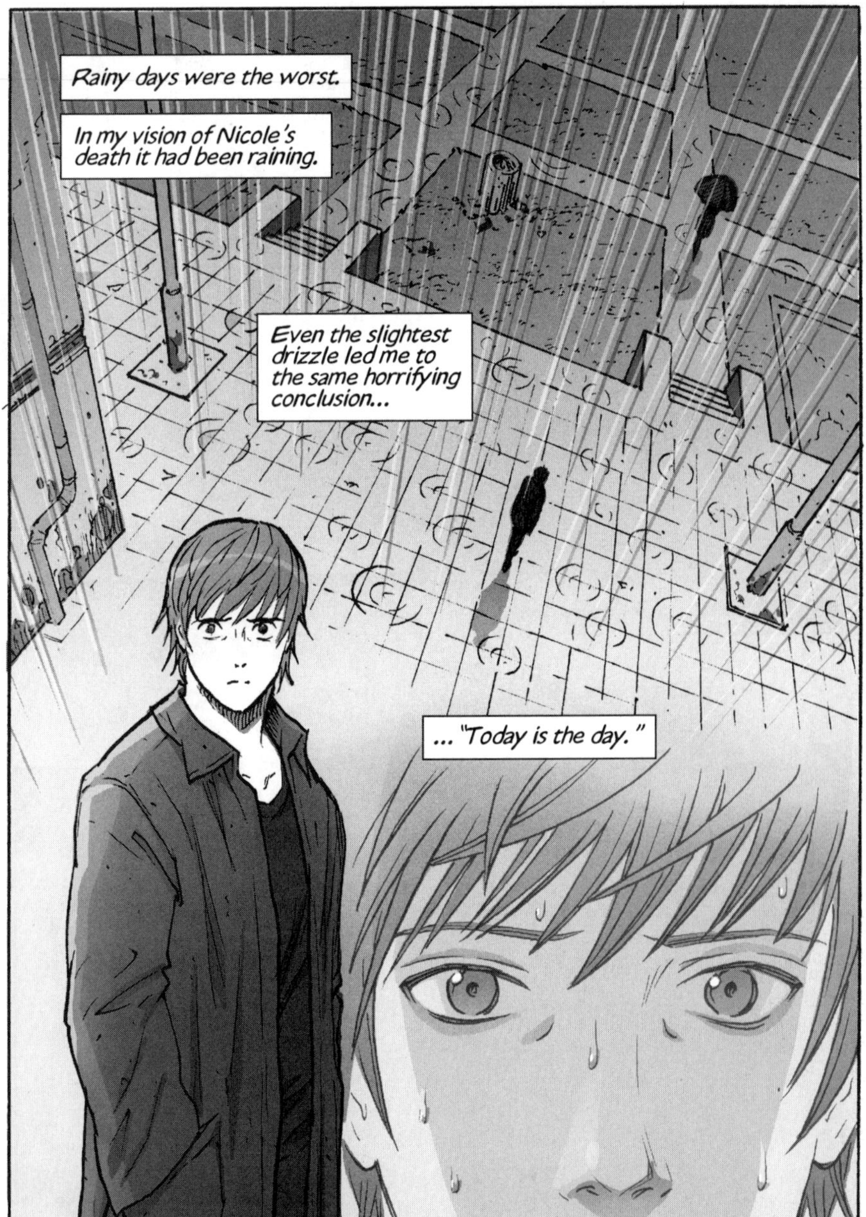
Rainy days were the worst.
In my vision of Nicole's death it had been raining.
Even the slightest drizzle led me to the same horrifying conclusion...
..."Today is the day."

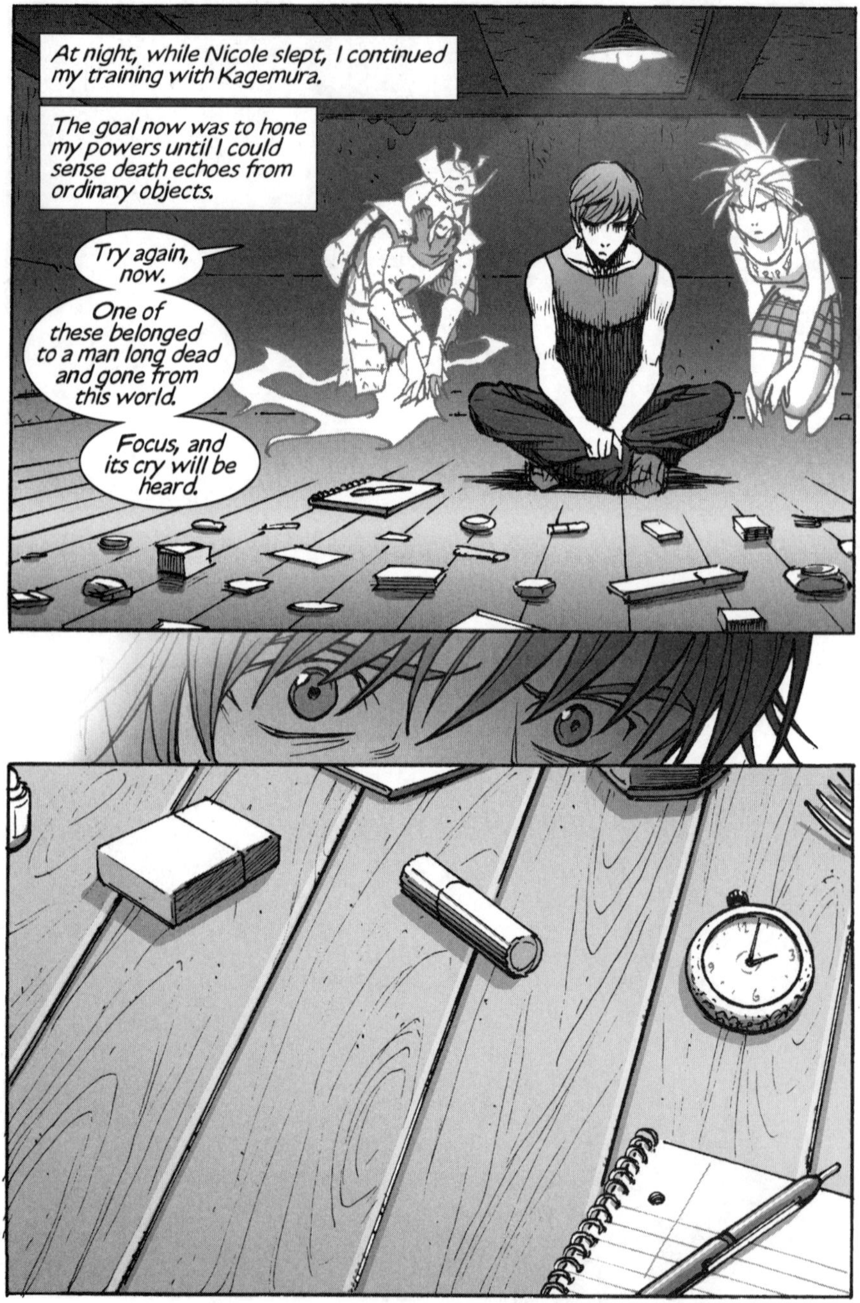
At night, while Nicole slept, I continued my training with Kagemura.
The goal now was to hone my powers until I could sense death echoes from ordinary objects.
Try again, now.
One of these belonged to a man long dead and gone from this world.
Focus, and its cry will be heard.

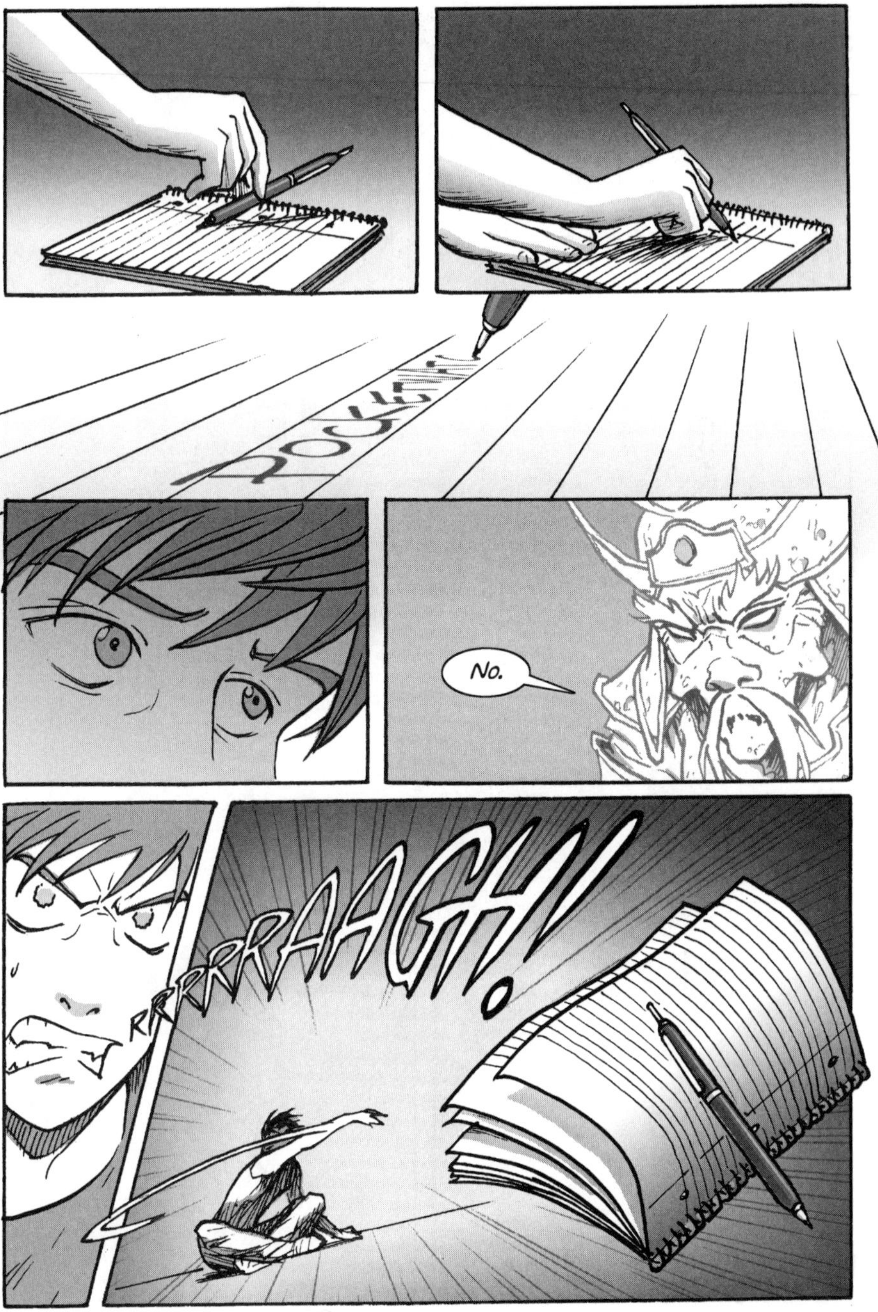
No.
RRRRRRRAAGH!!

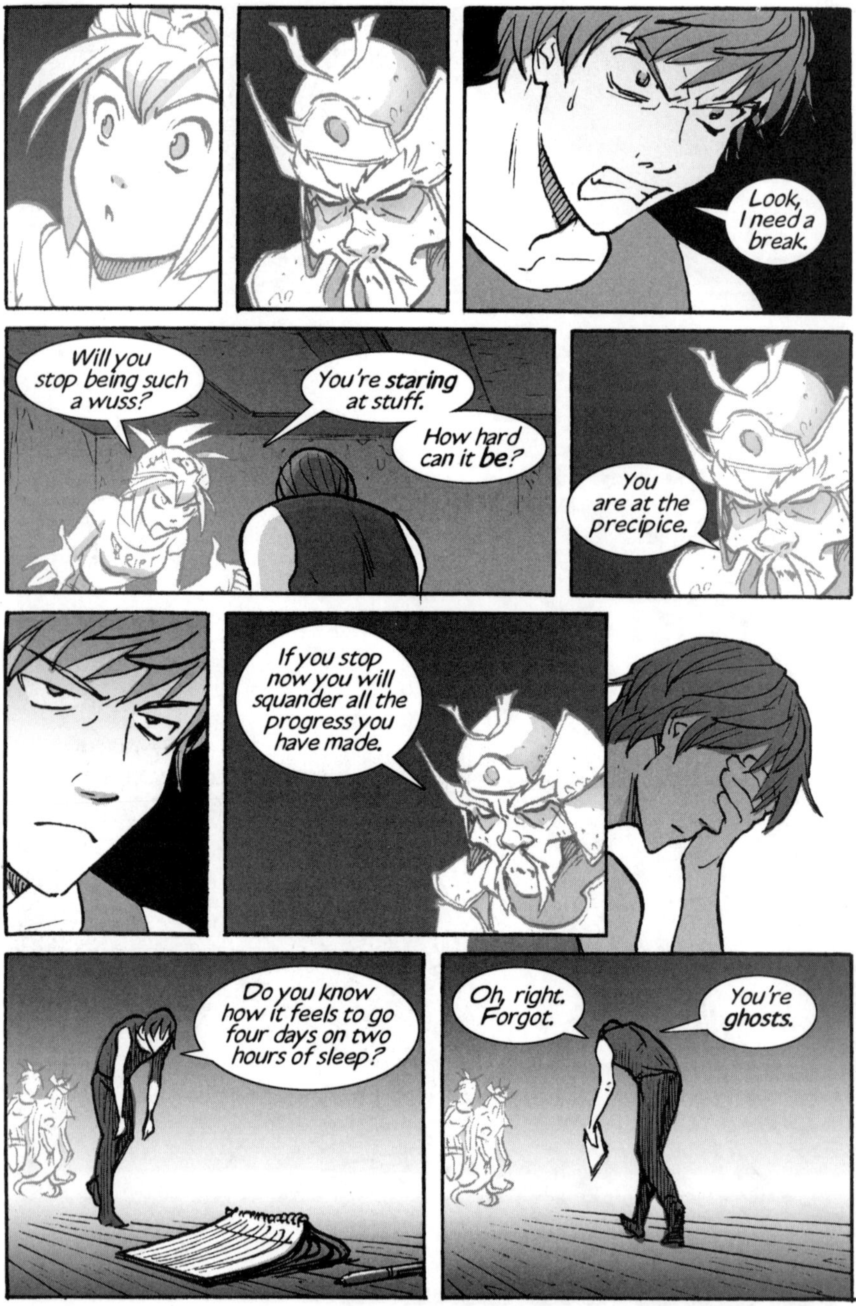
Look, I need a break.
Will you stop being such a wuss?
You're staring at stuff.
How hard can it be?
You are at the precipice.
If you stop now you will squander all the progress you have made.
Do you know how it feels to go four days on two hours of sleep?
Oh, right. Forgot.
You're ghosts.

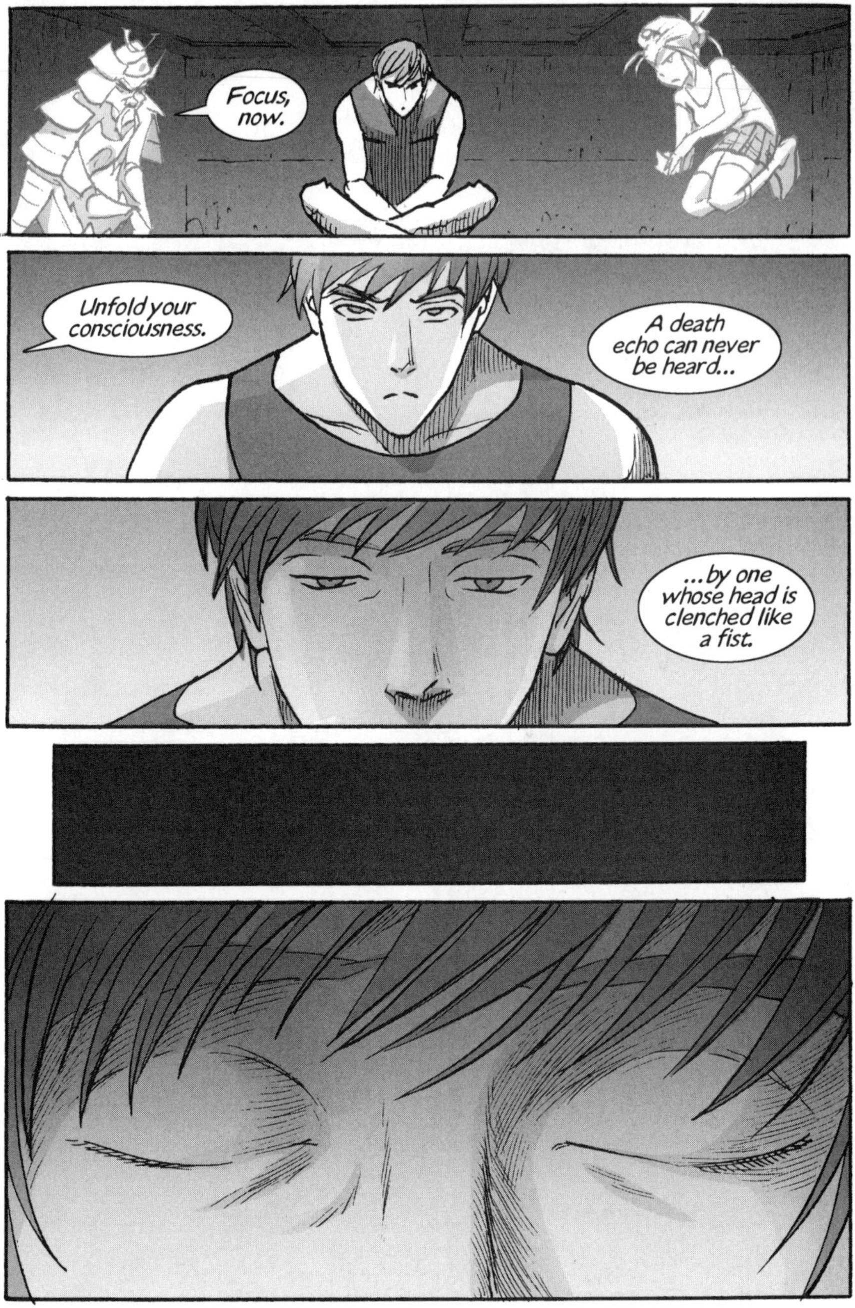
Focus, now.
Unfold your consciousness.
A death echo can never be heard...
...by one whose head is clenched like a fist.

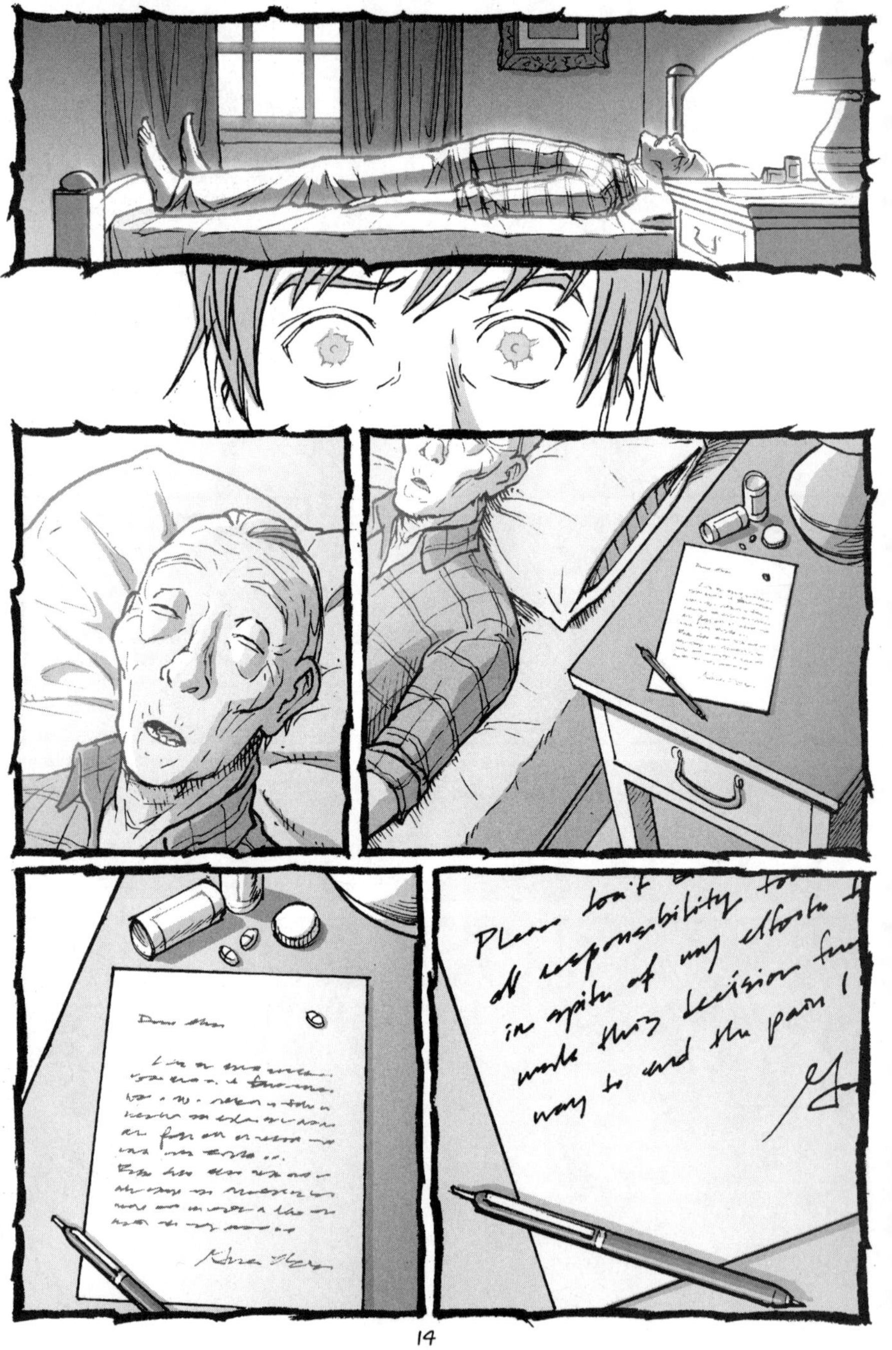

Please don't
all responsibility
in spite of my efforts
made this decision
way to end the pain

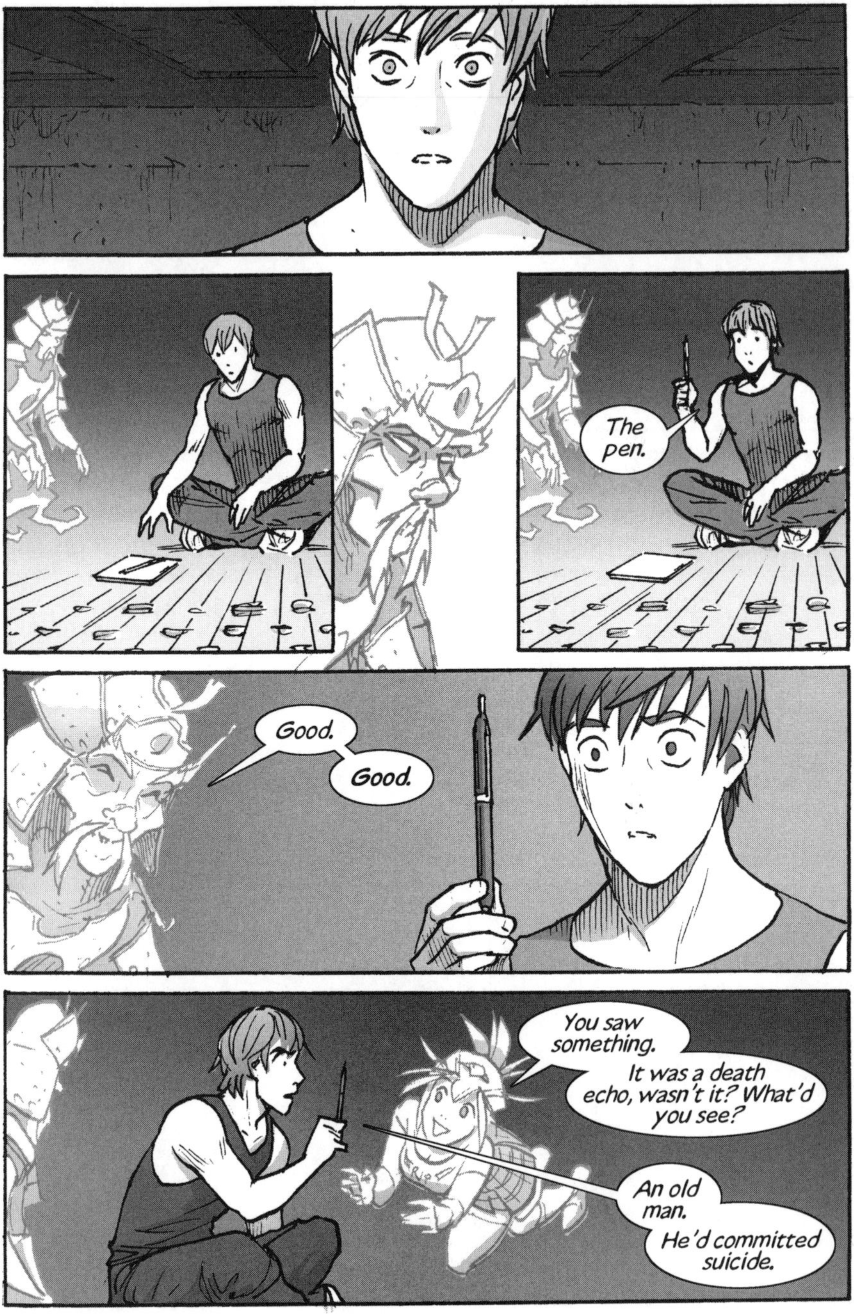
The pen.
Good.
Good.
You saw something.
It was a death echo, wasn't it? What'd you see?
An old man.
He'd committed suicide.

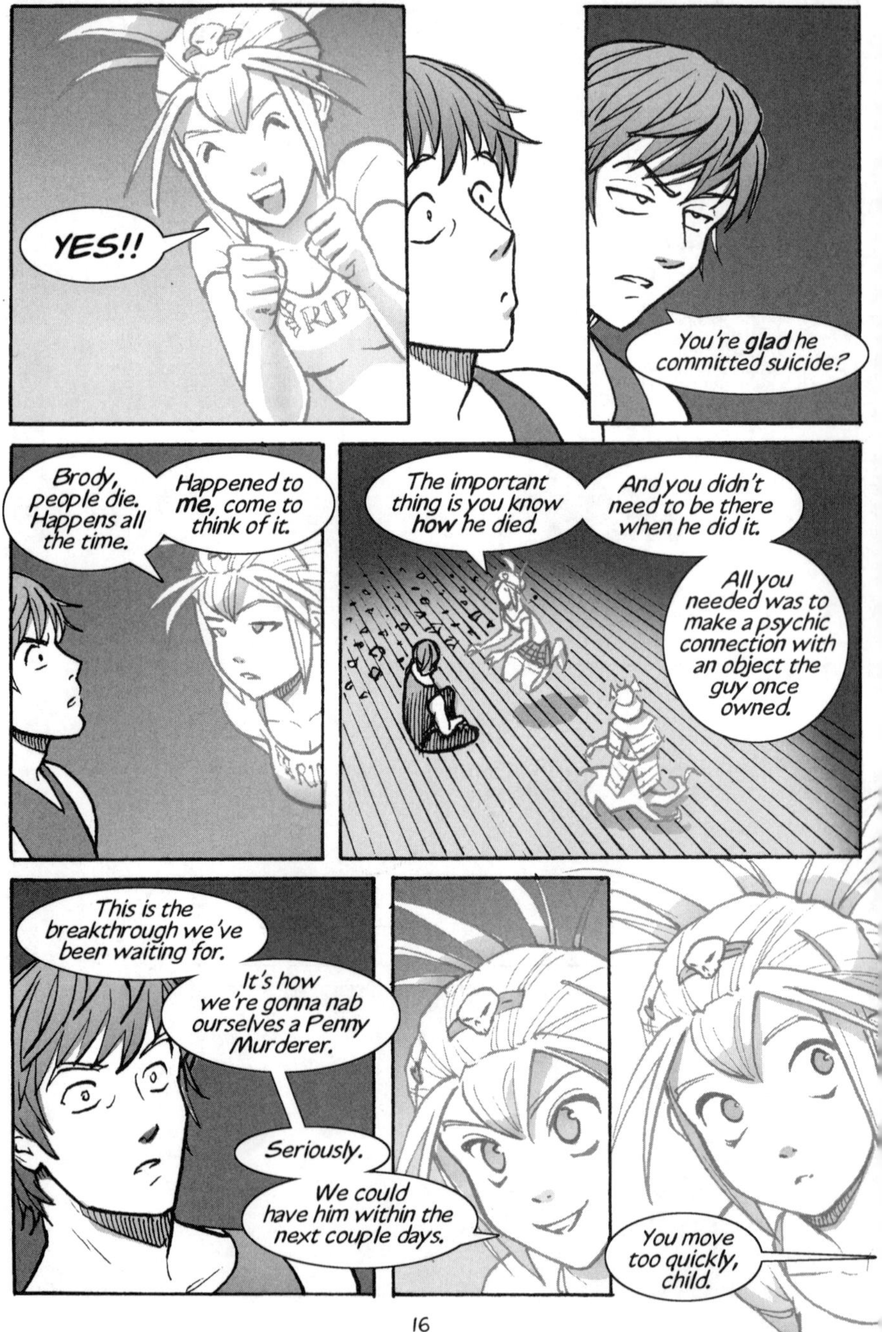
YES!!
You're **glad** he committed suicide?
Brody, people die. Happens all the time.
Happened to **me**, come to think of it.
The important thing is you know **how** he died.
And you didn't need to be there when he did it.
All you needed was to make a psychic connection with an object the guy once owned.
This is the breakthrough we've been waiting for.
It's how we're gonna nab ourselves a Penny Murderer.
Seriously.
We could have him within the next couple days.
You move too quickly, child.

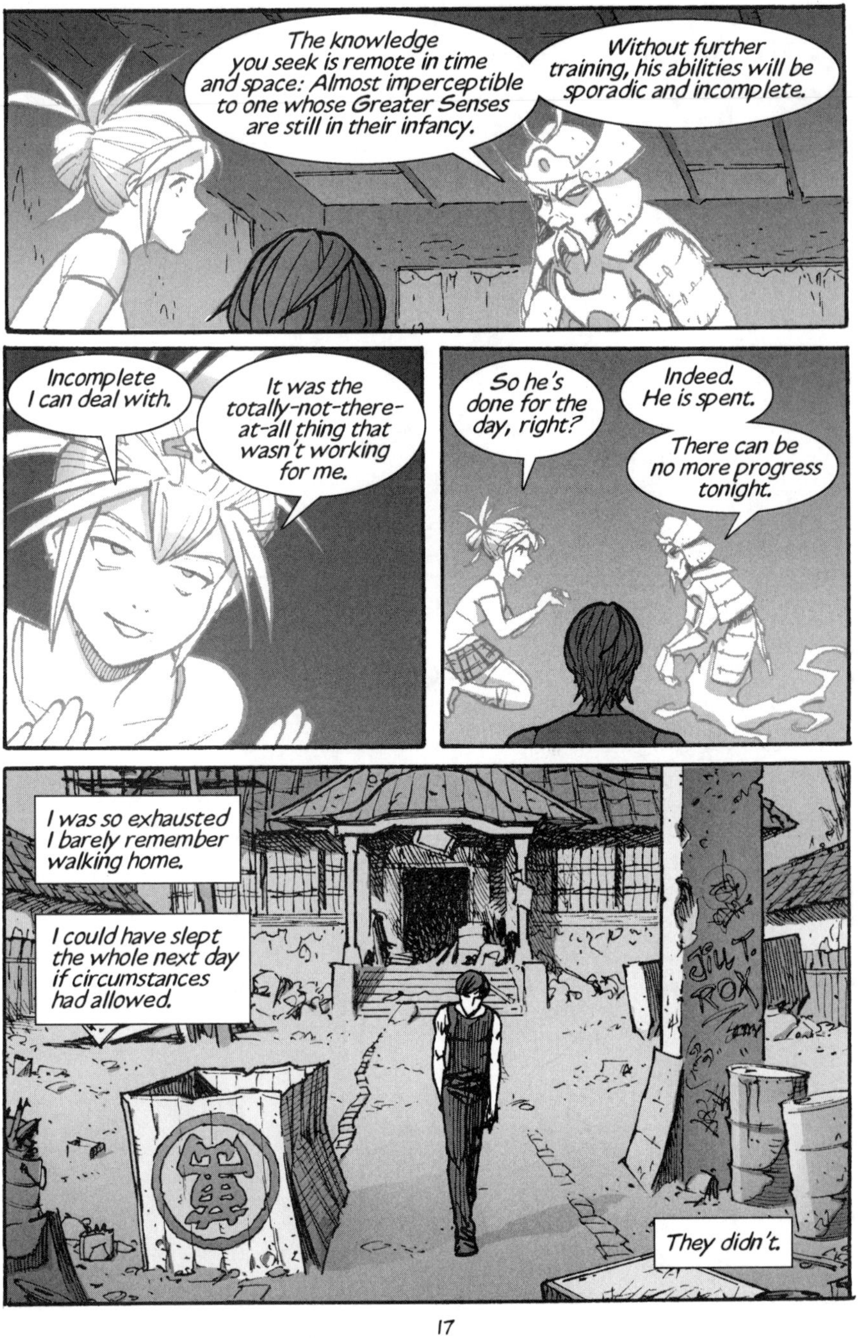

The knowledge you seek is remote in time and space: Almost imperceptible to one whose Greater Senses are still in their infancy.
Without further training, his abilities will be sporadic and incomplete.
Incomplete I can deal with.
It was the totally-not-there-at-all thing that wasn't working for me.
So he's done for the day, right?
Indeed. He is spent.
There can be no more progress tonight.
I was so exhausted I barely remember walking home.
I could have slept the whole next day if circumstances had allowed.
JILL T. ROX
They didn't.

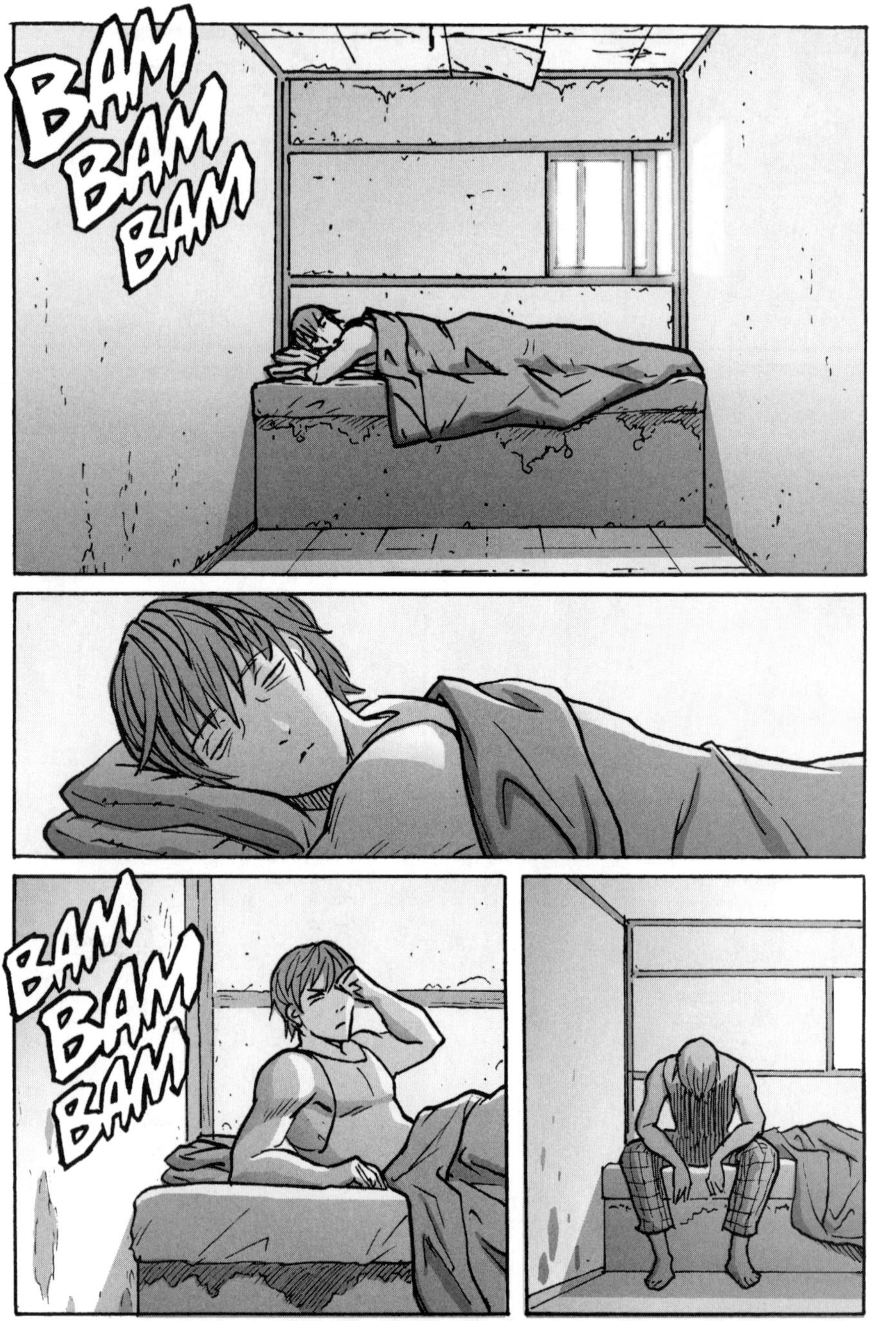
BAM
BAM
BAM
BAM
BAM
BAM

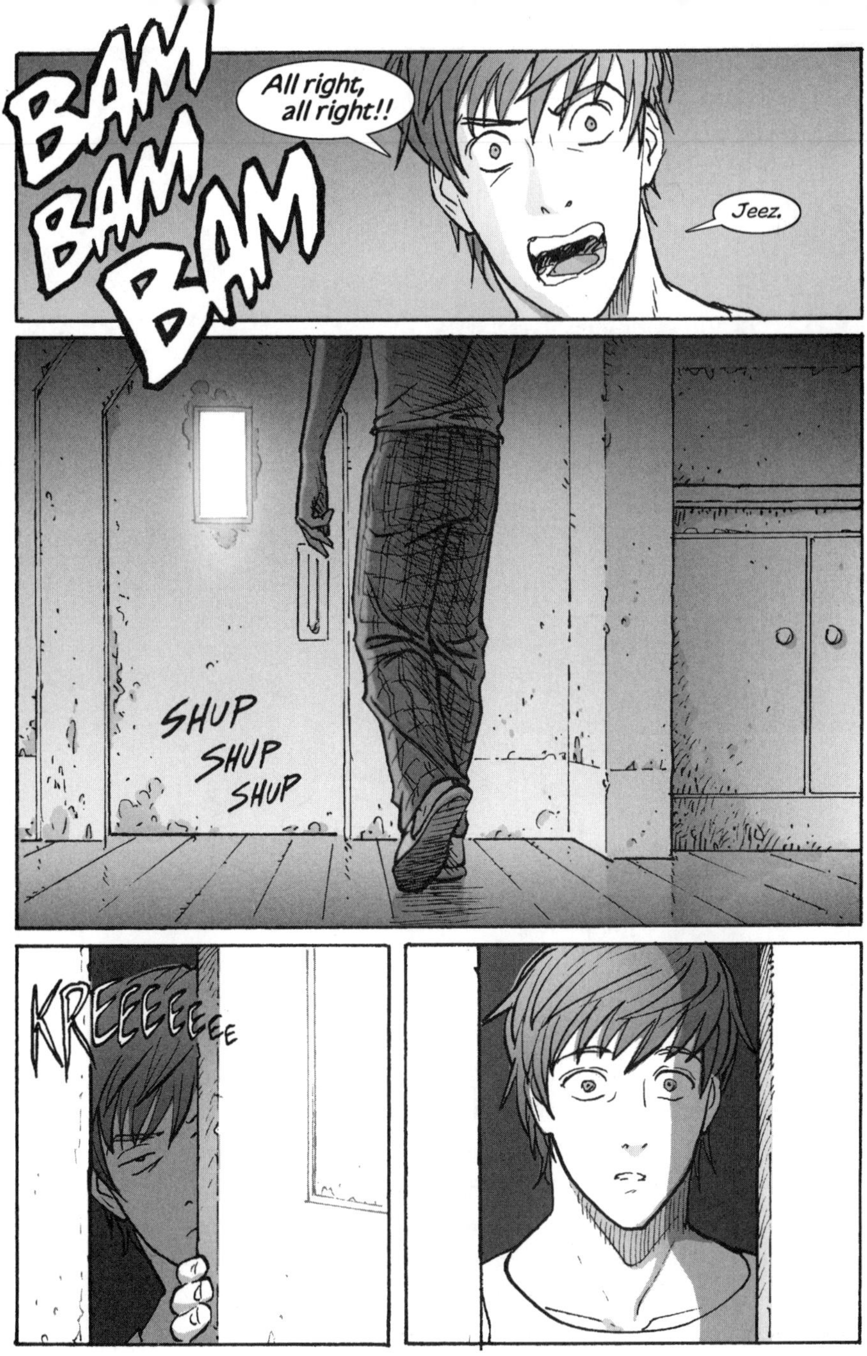
BAM
BAM
BAM
All right, all right!!
Jeez.
SHUP
SHUP
SHUP
KREEEEEEE

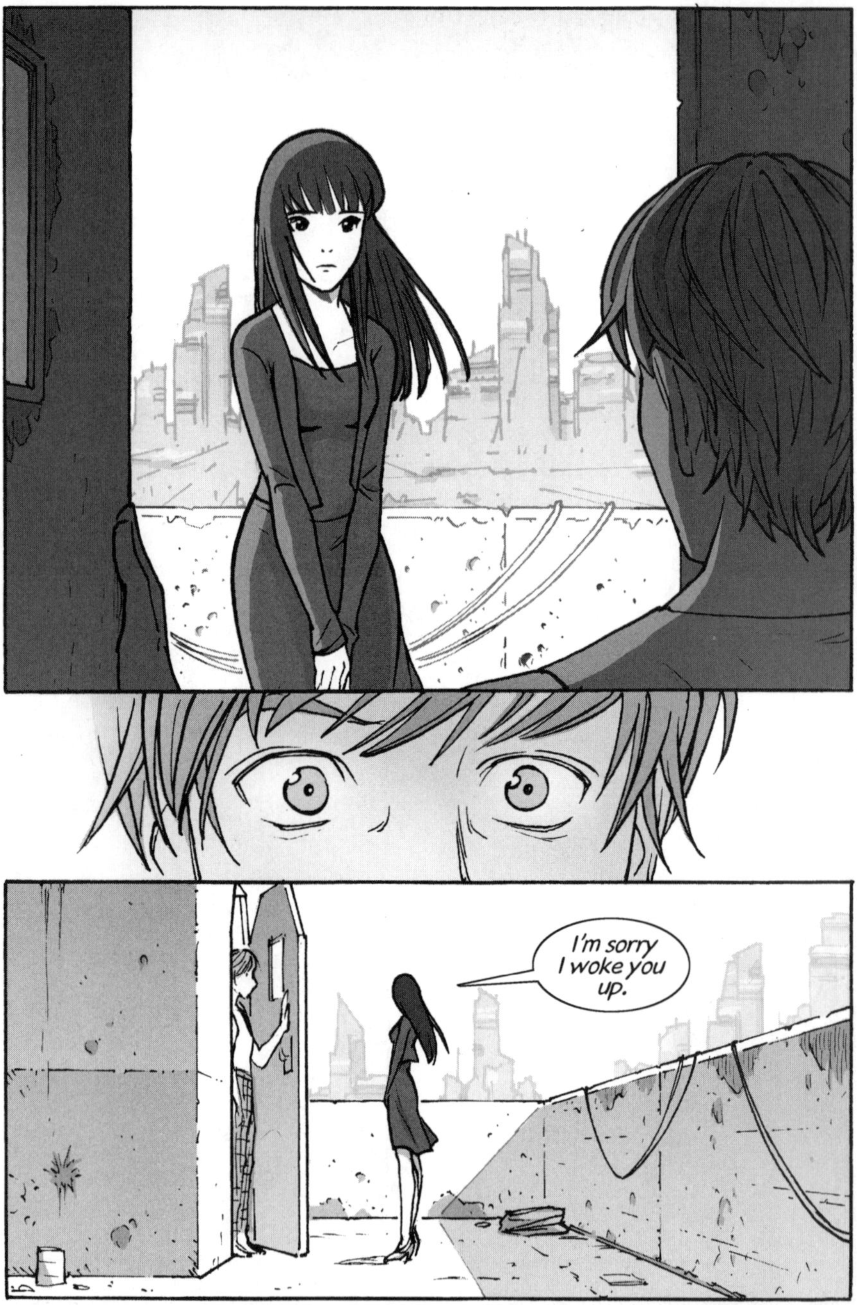
I'm sorry I woke you up.

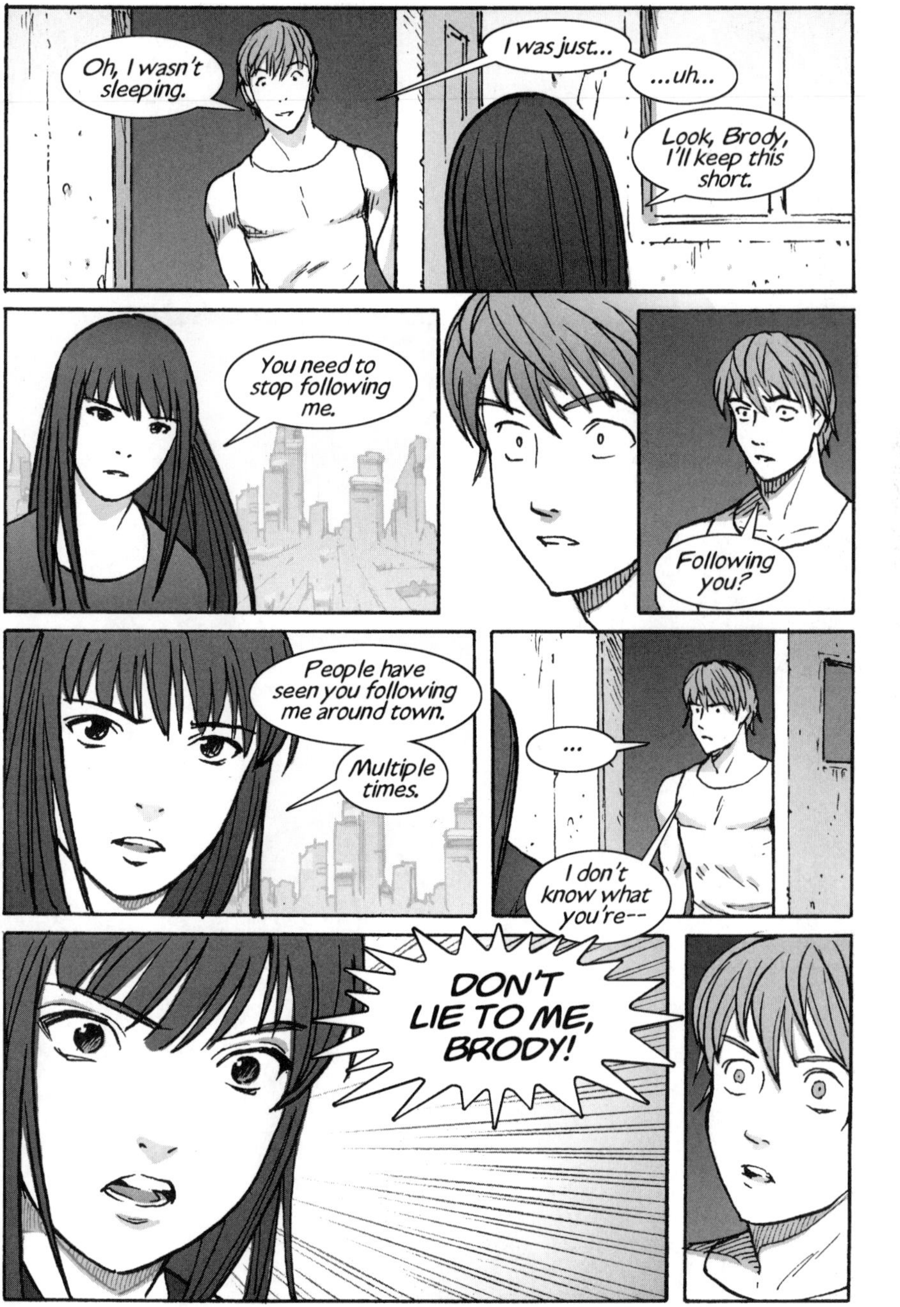
Oh, I wasn't sleeping.
I was just...
...uh...
Look, Brody, I'll keep this short.
You need to stop following me.
Following you?
People have seen you following me around town.
Multiple times.
...
I don't know what you're--
DON'T LIE TO ME, BRODY!

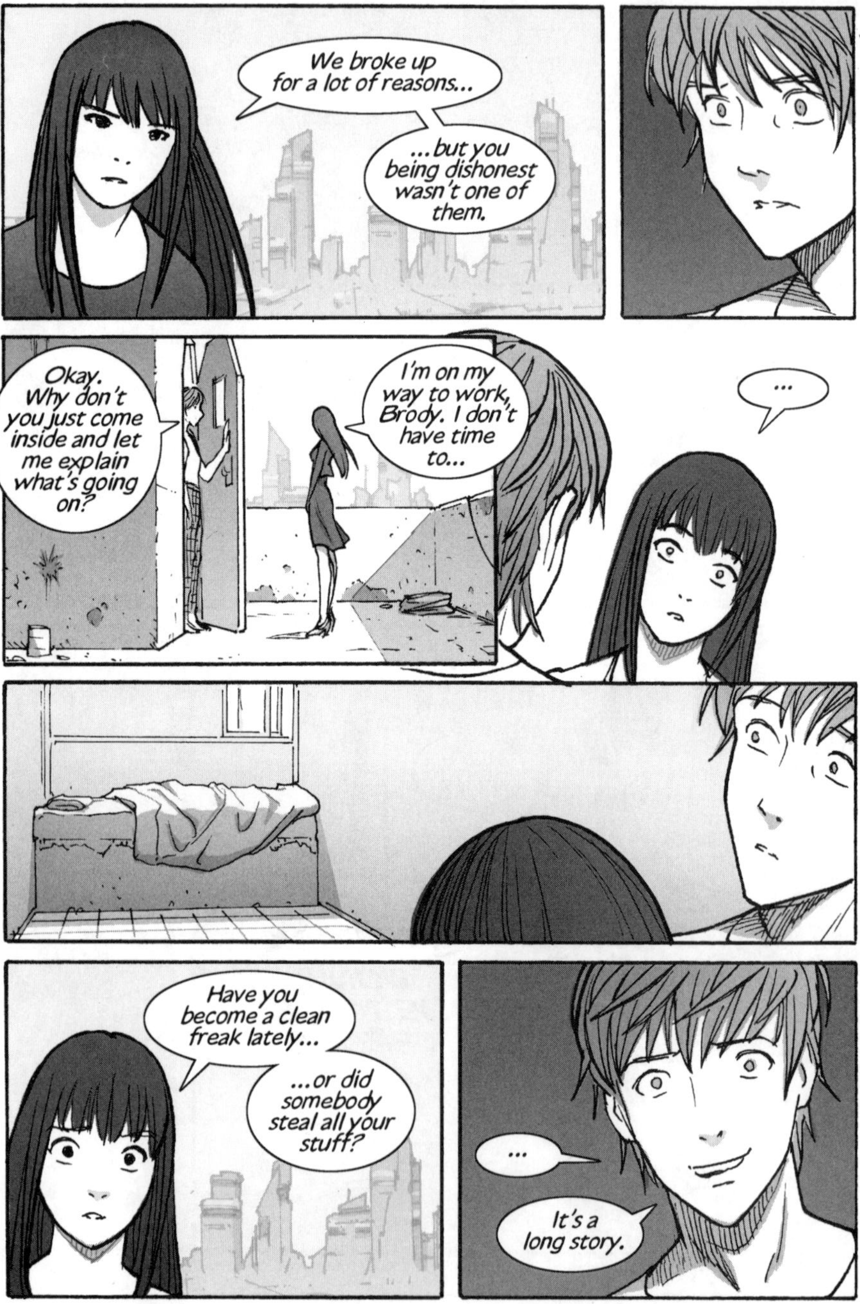
We broke up for a lot of reasons...
...but you being dishonest wasn't one of them.
Okay. Why don't you just come inside and let me explain what's going on?
I'm on my way to work, Brody. I don't have time to...
...
Have you become a clean freak lately...
...or did somebody steal all your stuff?
...
It's a long story.

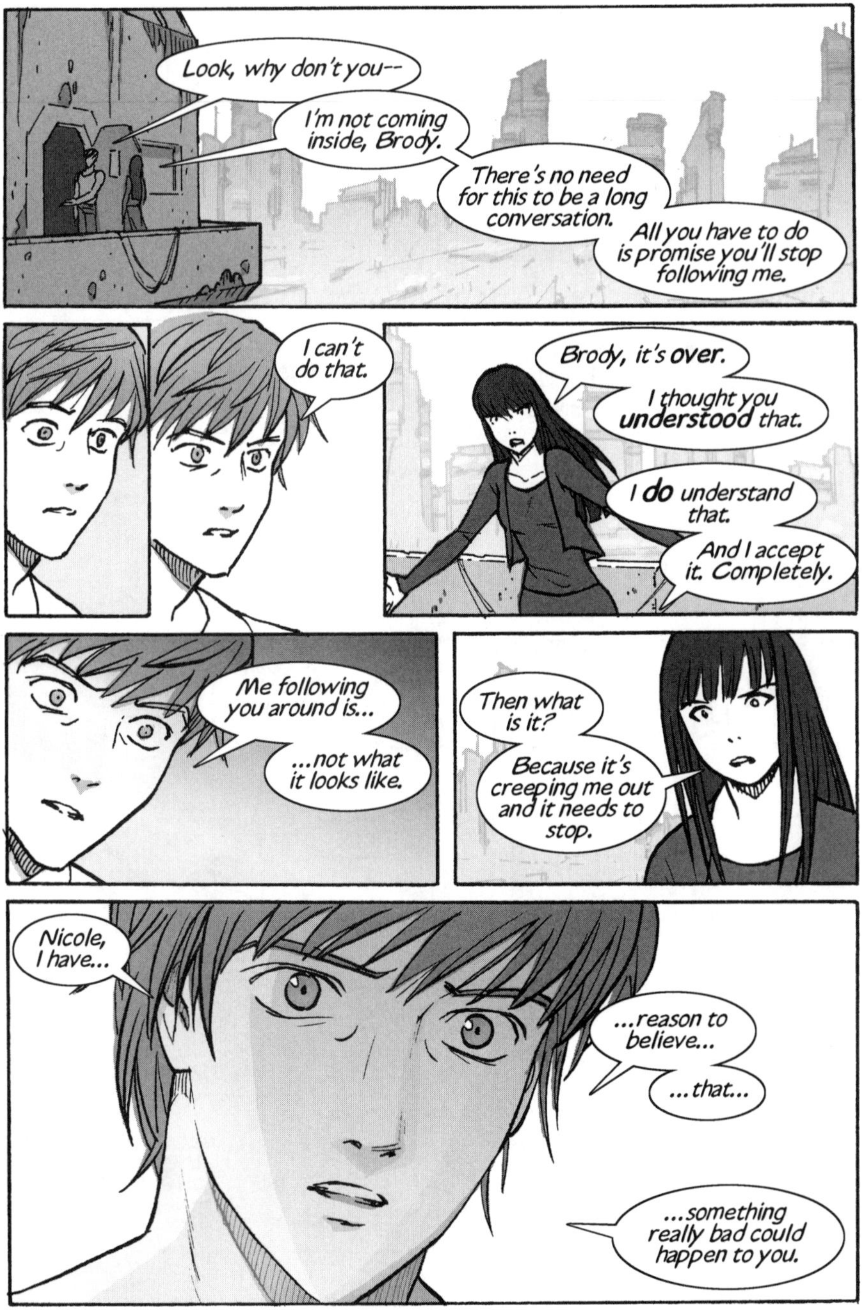
Look, why don't you--
I'm not coming inside, Brody.
There's no need for this to be a long conversation.
All you have to do is promise you'll stop following me.
I can't do that.
Brody, it's **over**.
I thought you **understood** that.
I **do** understand that.
And I accept it. Completely.
Me following you around is...
...not what it looks like.
Then what is it?
Because it's creeping me out and it needs to stop.
Nicole, I have...
...reason to believe...
...that...
...something really bad could happen to you.

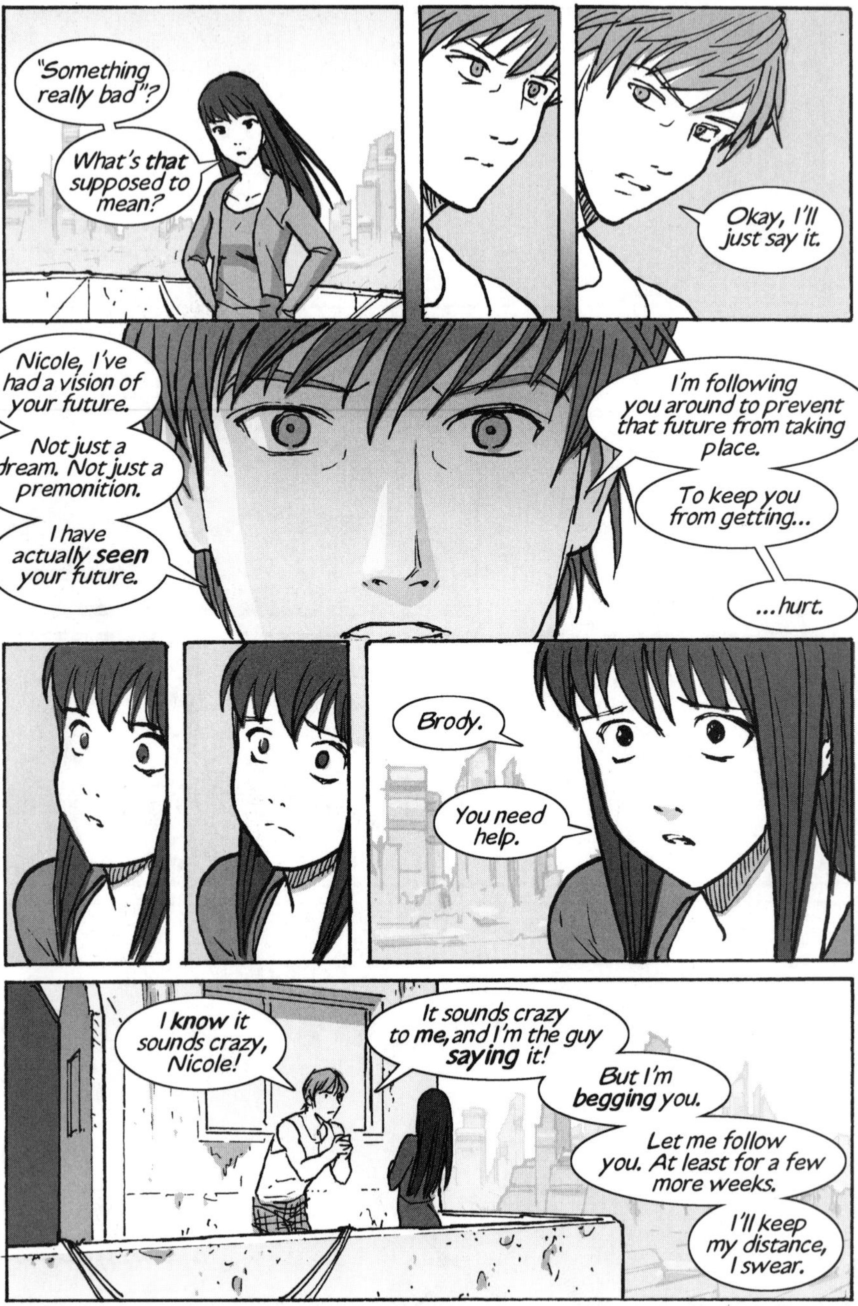

"Something really bad"?
What's that supposed to mean?
Okay, I'll just say it.
Nicole, I've had a vision of your future.
Not just a dream. Not just a premonition.
I have actually **seen** your future.
I'm following you around to prevent that future from taking place.
To keep you from getting...
...hurt.
Brody.
You need help.
I **know** it sounds crazy, Nicole!
It sounds crazy to **me**, and I'm the guy **saying** it!
But I'm **begging** you.
Let me follow you. At least for a few more weeks.
I'll keep my distance, I swear.

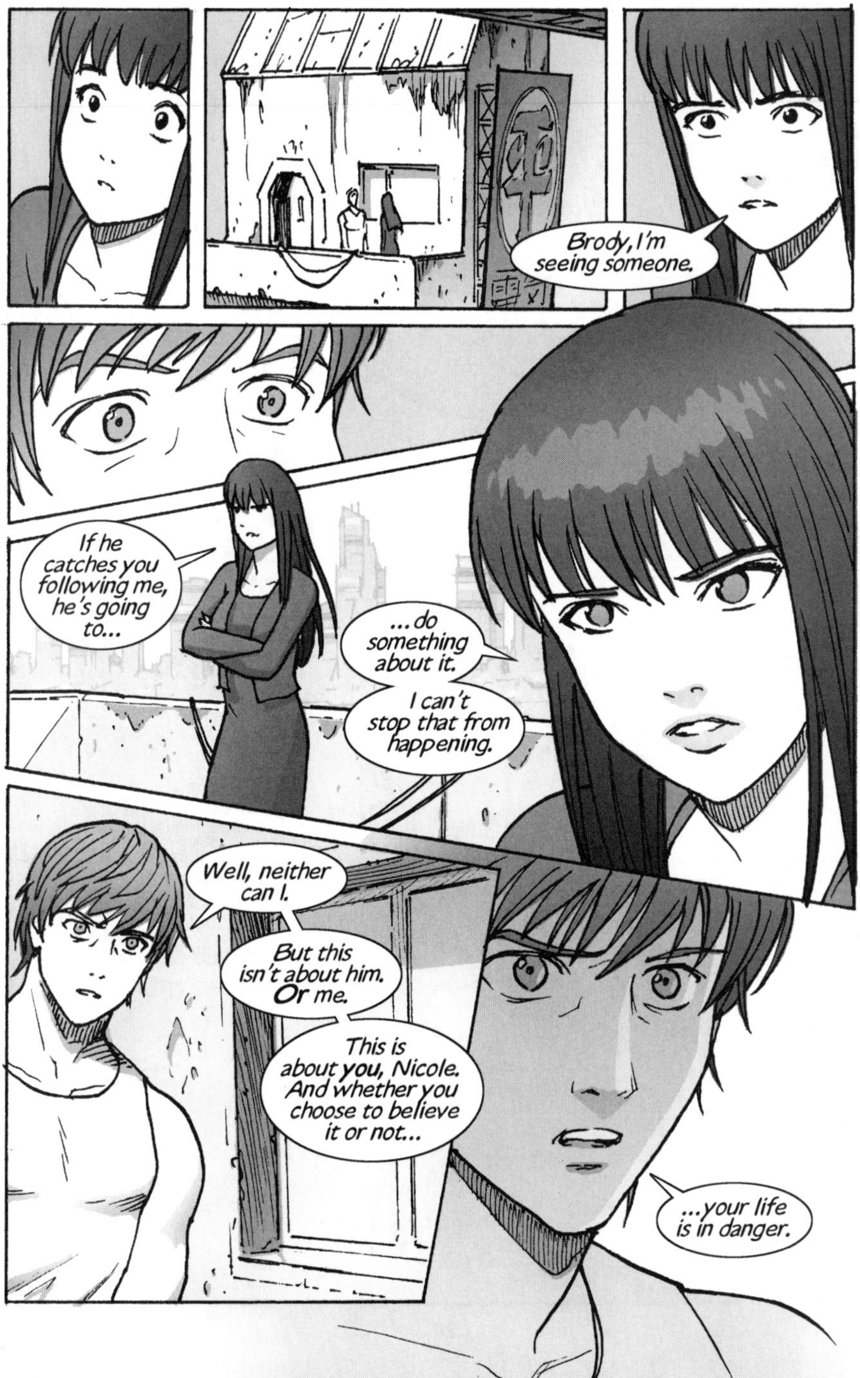
Brody, I'm seeing someone.
If he catches you following me, he's going to...
...do something about it.
I can't stop that from happening.
Well, neither can I.
But this isn't about him. Or me.
This is about you, Nicole. And whether you choose to believe it or not...
...your life is in danger.

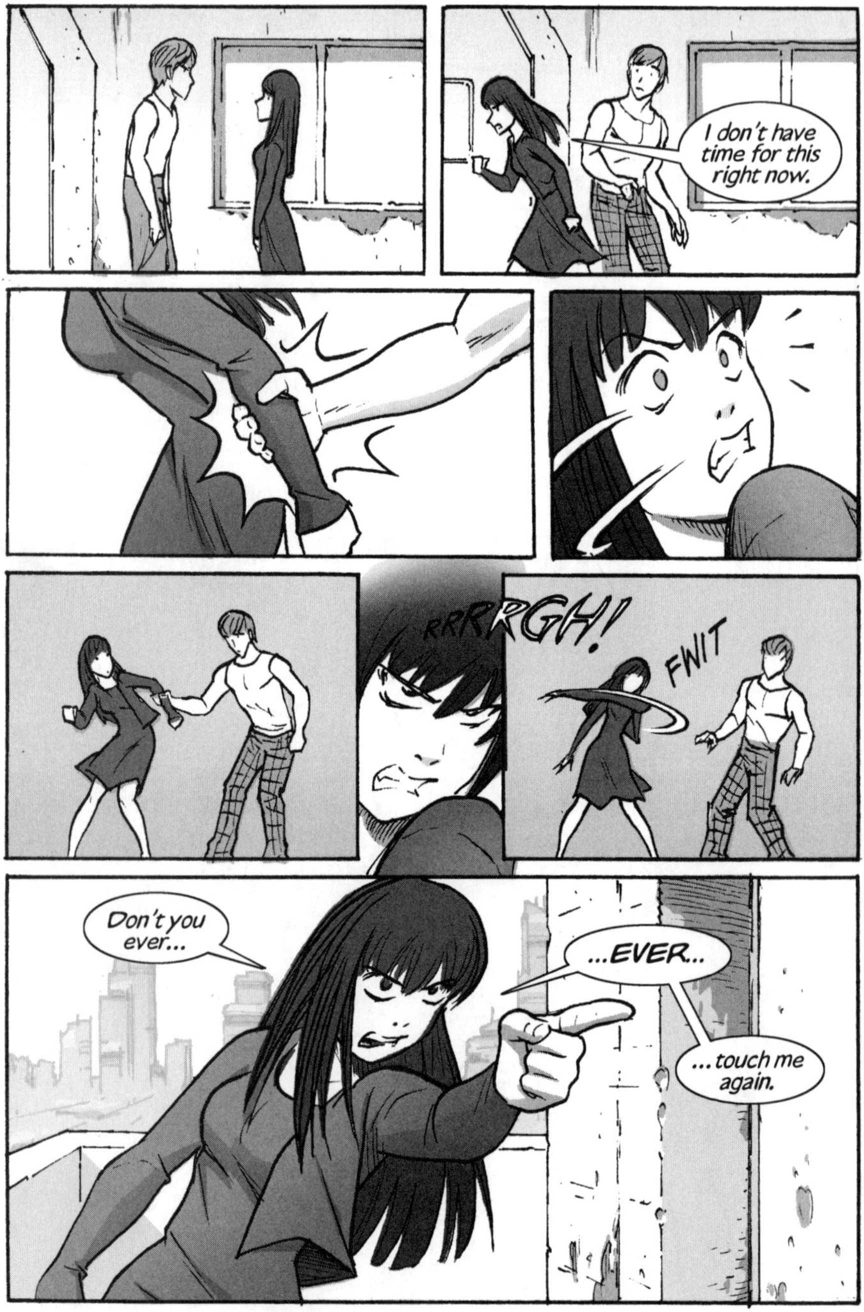
I don't have time for this right now.
RRRRGH!
FWIT
Don't you ever...
...EVER...
...touch me again.

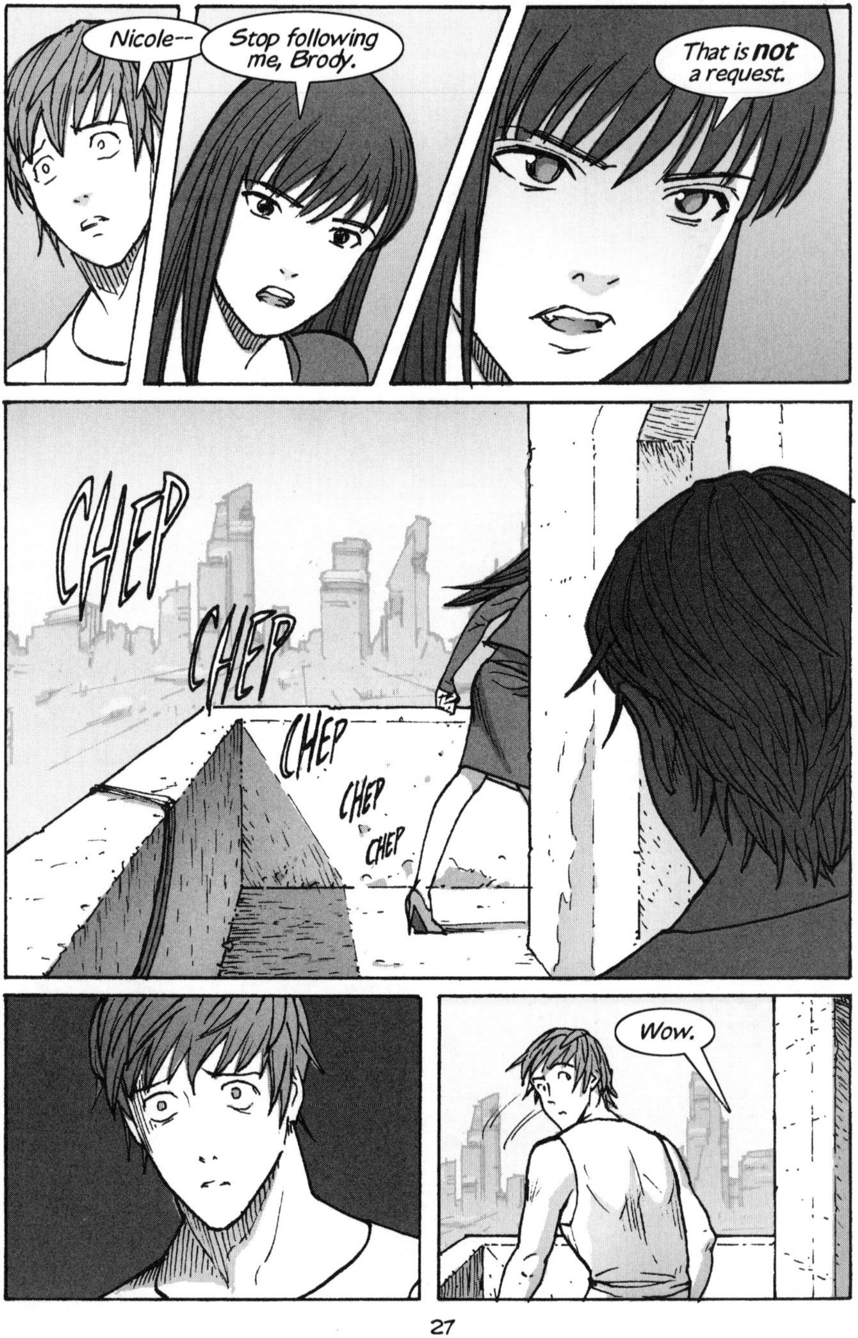
Nicole--
Stop following me, Brody.
That is **not** a request.
CHEP
CHEP
CHEP
CHEP
CHEP
Wow.

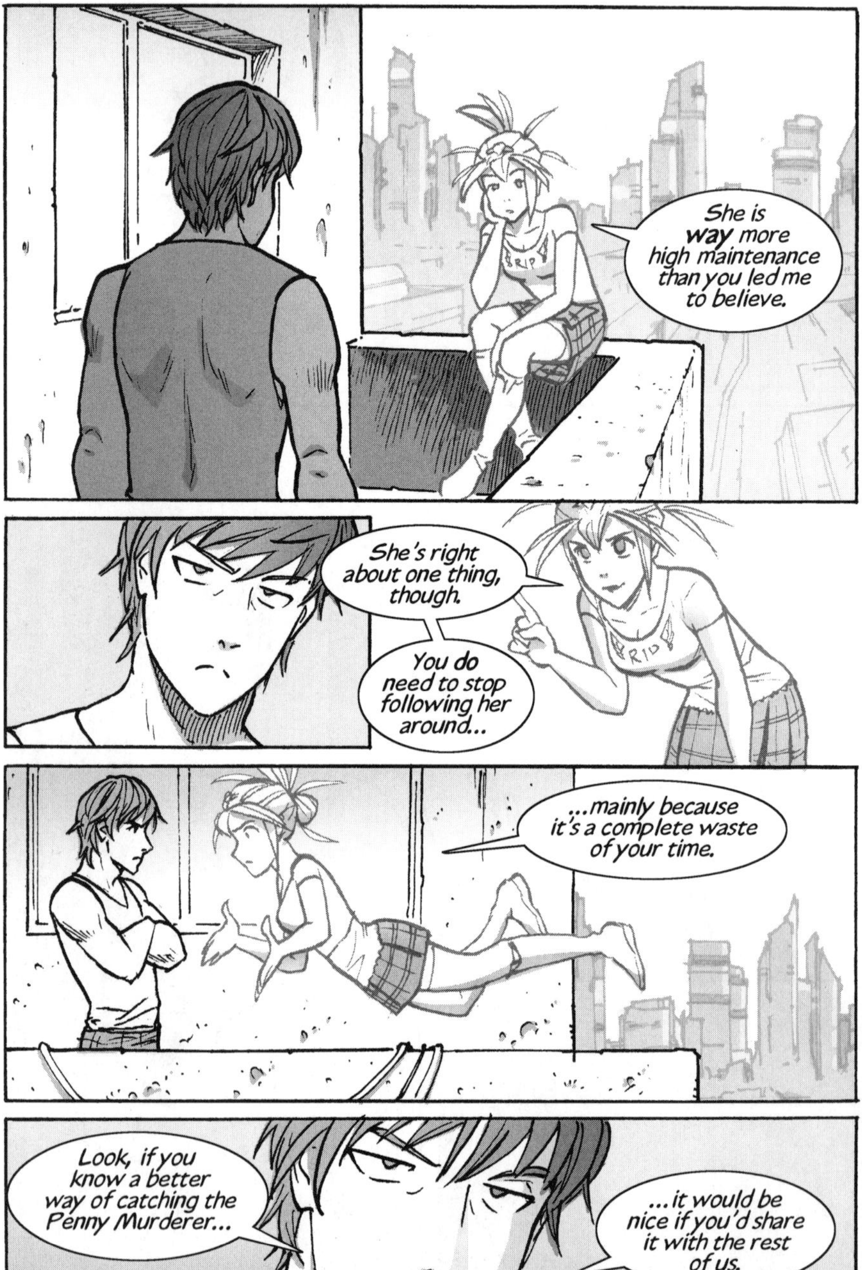
She is **way** more high maintenance than you led me to believe.
She's right about one thing, though.
You **do** need to stop following her around...
...mainly because it's a complete waste of your time.
Look, if you know a better way of catching the Penny Murderer...
...it would be nice if you'd share it with the rest of us.

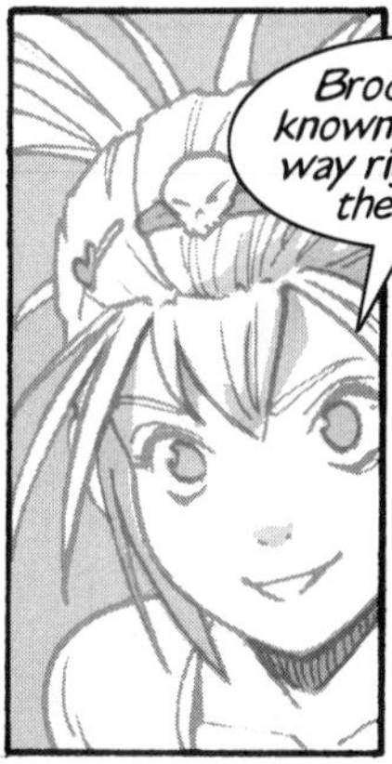
Brody, I've known a better way right from the start.
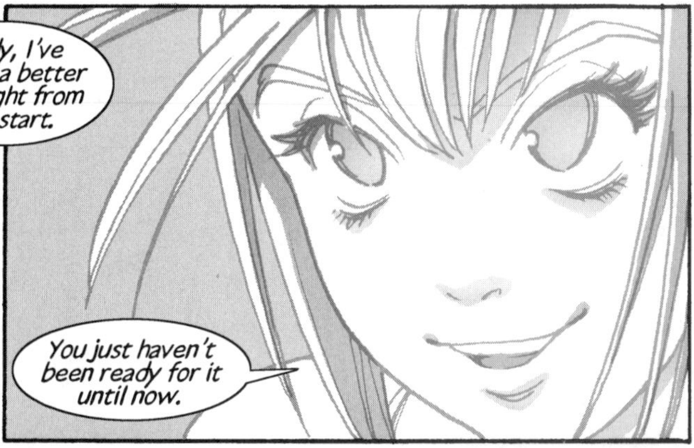
You just haven't been ready for it until now.
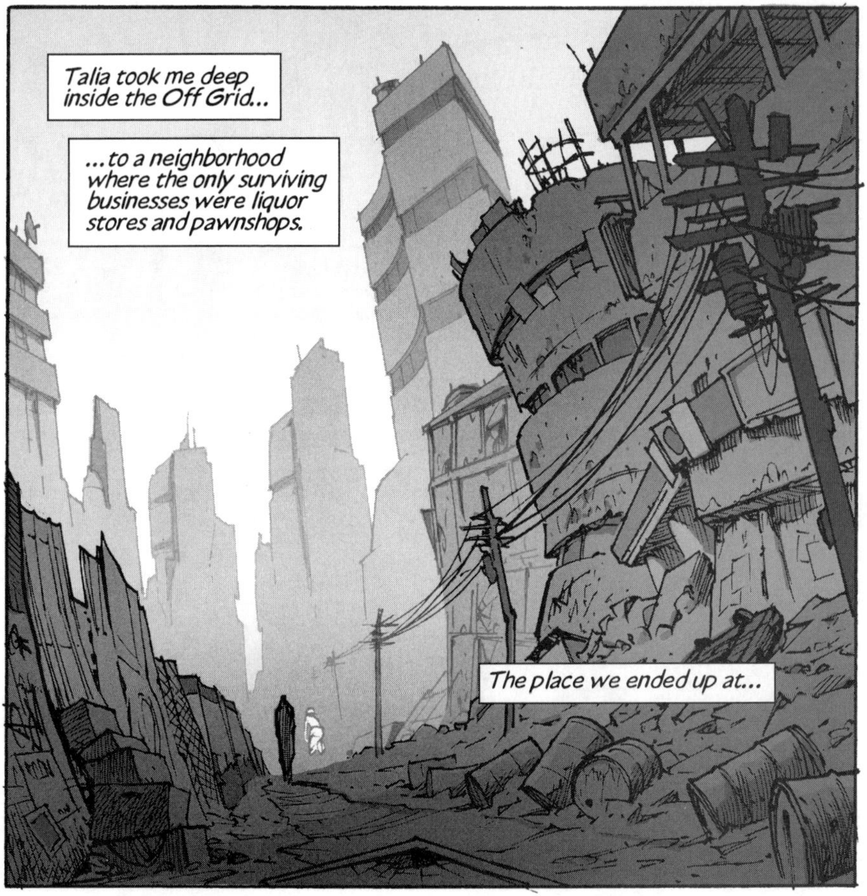
Talia took me deep inside the Off Grid...
...to a neighborhood where the only surviving businesses were liquor stores and pawnshops.
The place we ended up at...

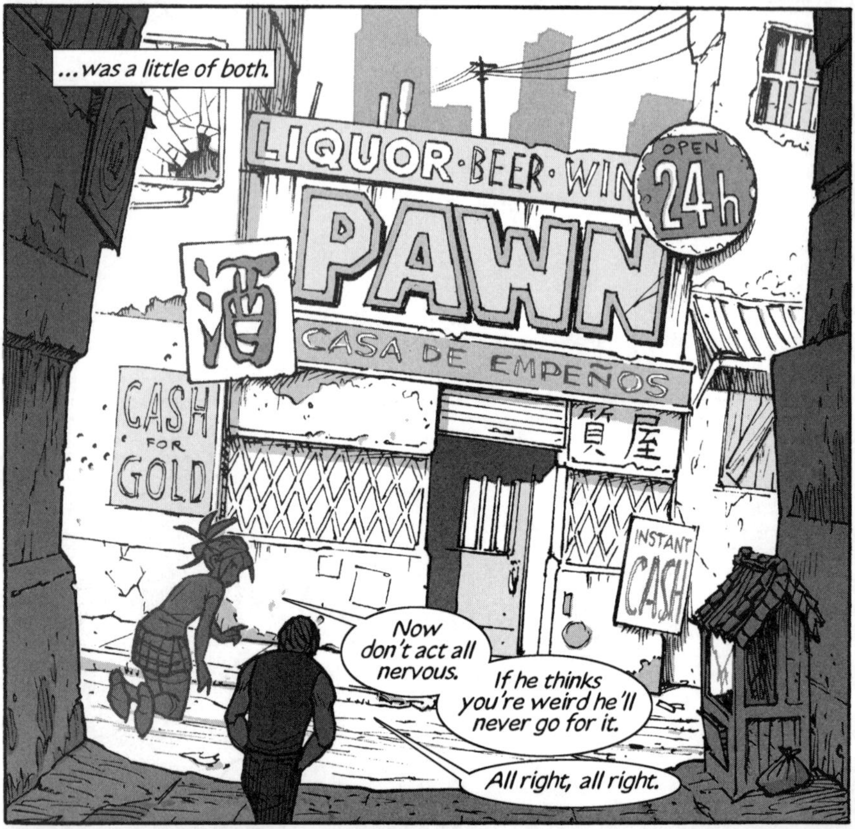
...was a little of both.
LIQUOR·BEER·WIN
OPEN
24h
PAWN
CASA DE EMPEÑOS
CASH FOR GOLD
質屋
INSTANT CASH
Now don't act all nervous.
If he thinks you're weird he'll never go for it.
All right, all right.

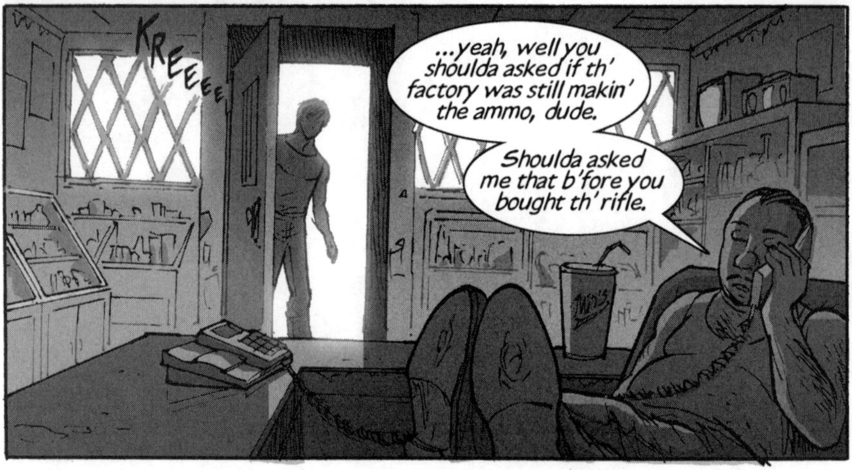
KREEEE
...yeah, well you shoulda asked if th' factory was still makin' the ammo, dude.
Shoulda asked me that b'fore you bought th' rifle.

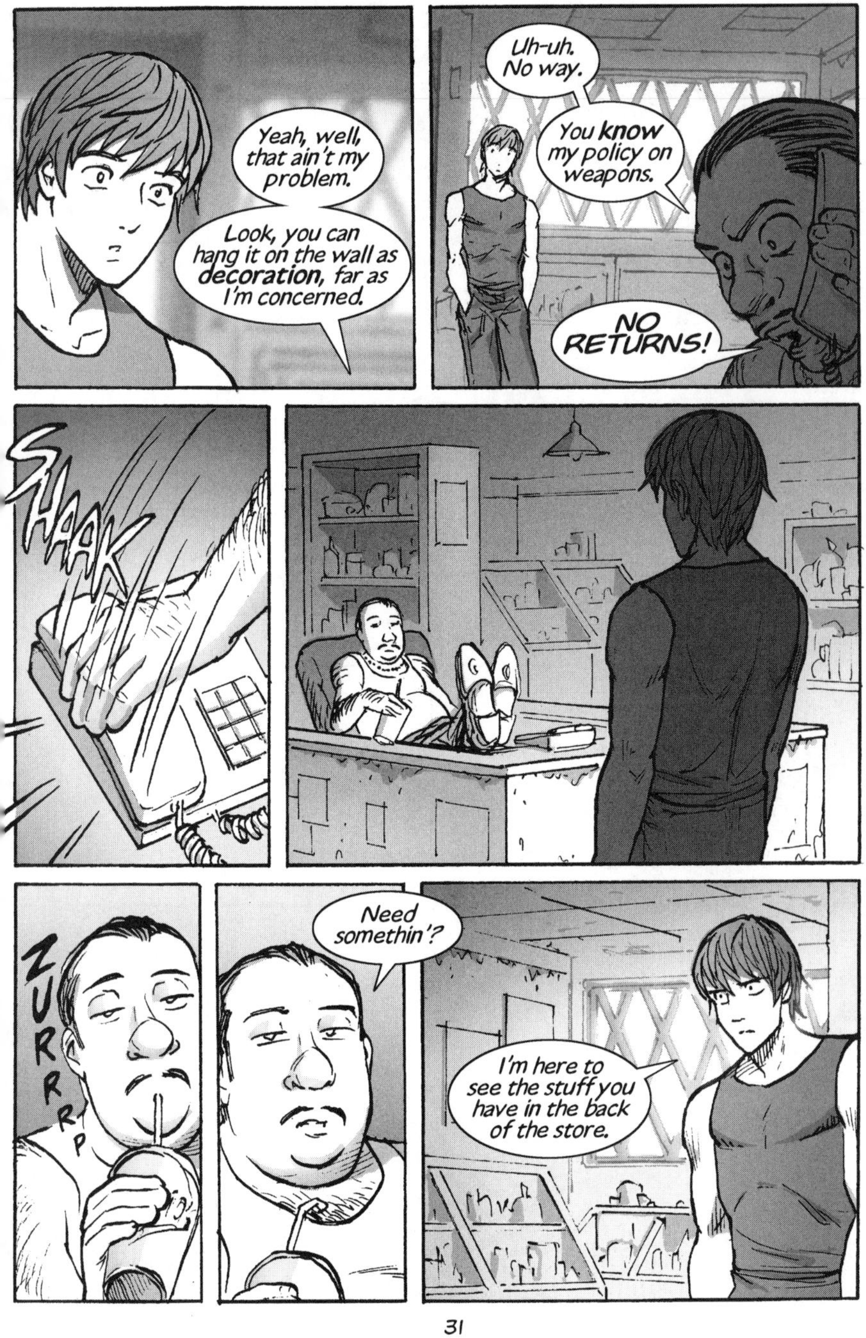
Yeah, well, that ain't my problem.
Look, you can hang it on the wall as **decoration**, far as I'm concerned.
Uh-uh. No way.
You **know** my policy on weapons.
NO RETURNS!
SHAAK
ZURRRP
Need somethin'?
I'm here to see the stuff you have in the back of the store.

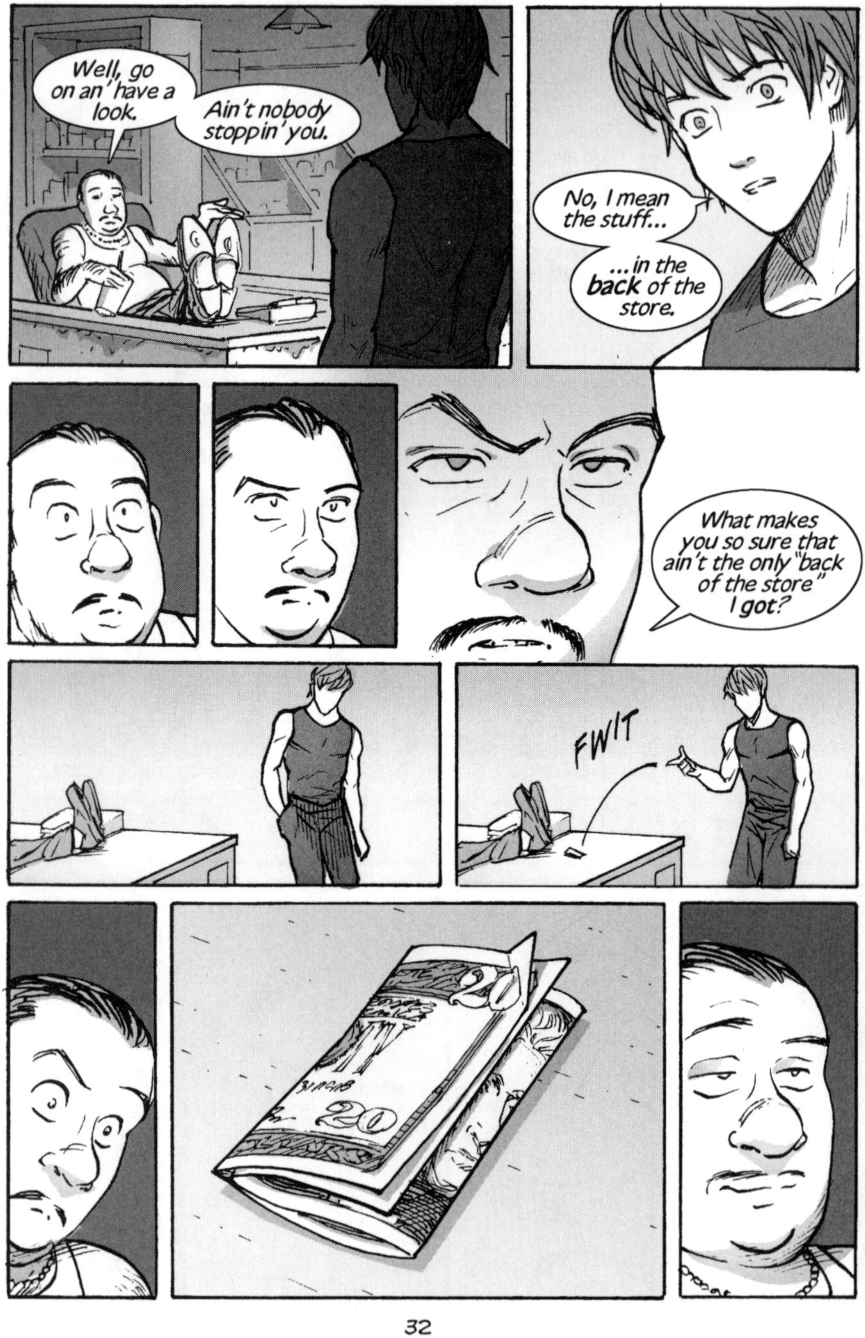
Well, go on an' have a look.
Ain't nobody stoppin' you.
No, I mean the stuff...
...in the **back** of the store.
What makes you so sure that ain't the only "back of the store" I **got**?
FWIT
20
20

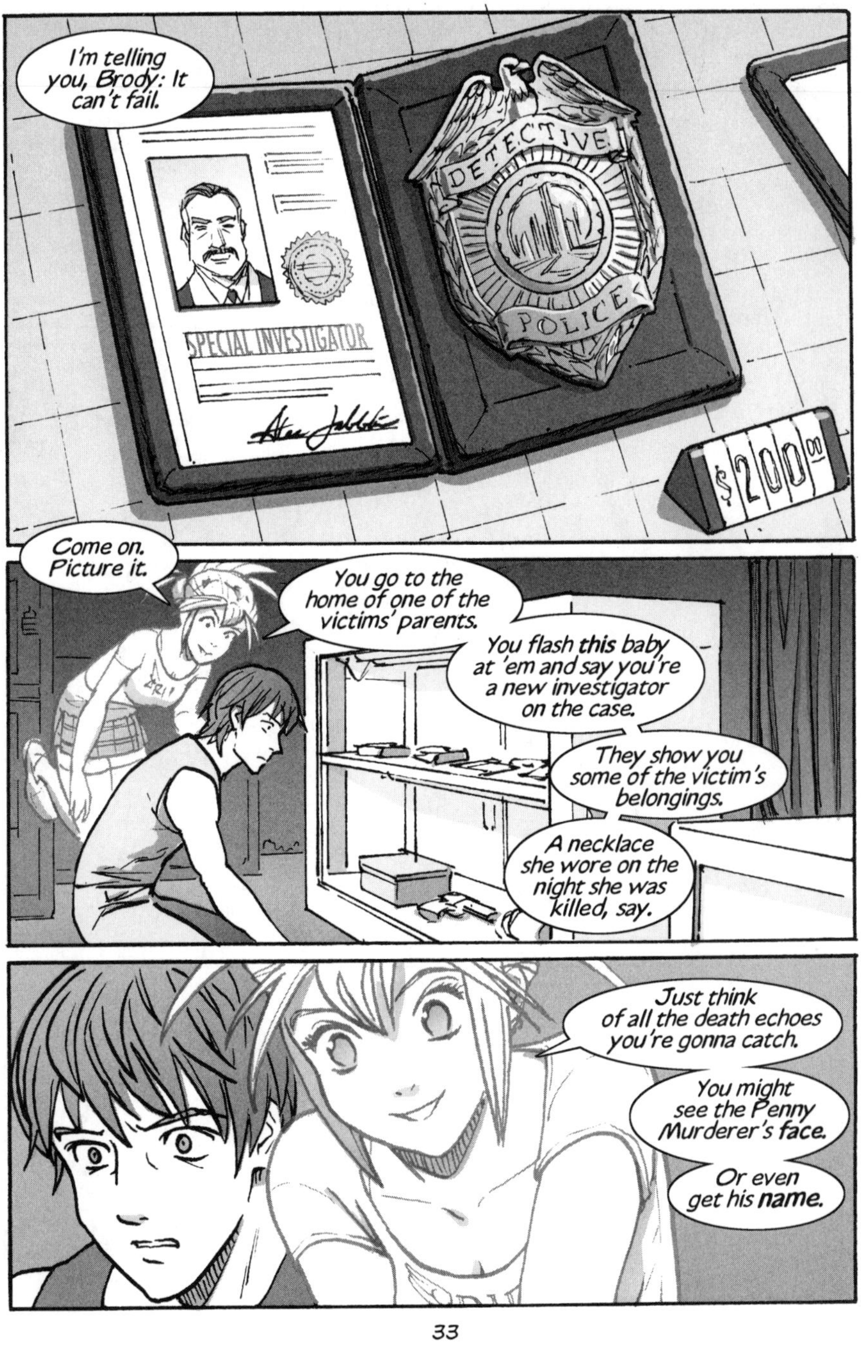
I'm telling you, Brody: It can't fail.
DETECTIVE
POLICE
SPECIAL INVESTIGATOR
$200.00
Come on. Picture it.
You go to the home of one of the victims' parents.
You flash **this** baby at 'em and say you're a new investigator on the case.
They show you some of the victim's belongings.
A necklace she wore on the night she was killed, say.
Just think of all the death echoes you're gonna catch.
You might see the Penny Murderer's **face**.
Or even get his **name**.

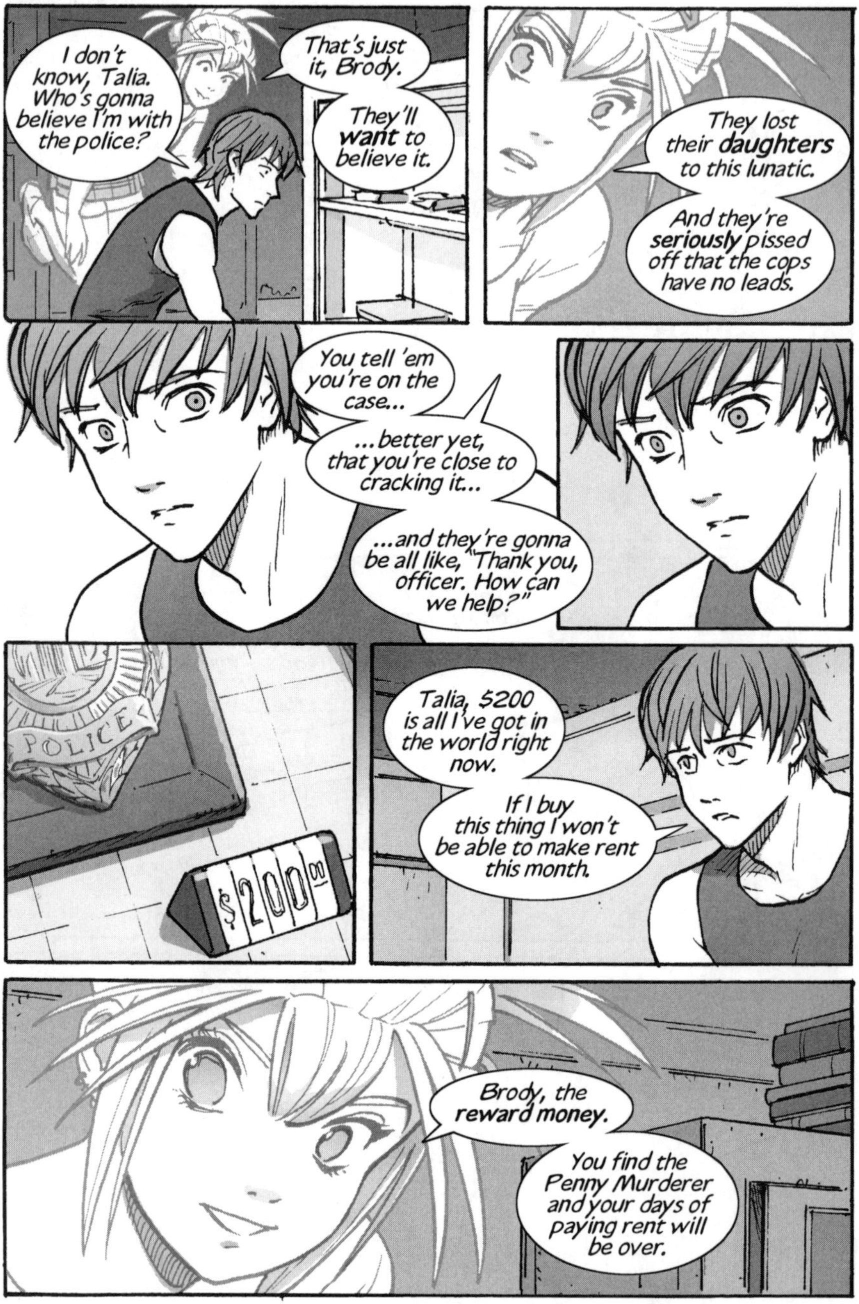
I don't know, Talia. Who's gonna believe I'm with the police?
That's just it, Brody.
They'll **want** to believe it.
They lost their **daughters** to this lunatic.
And they're **seriously** pissed off that the cops have no leads.
You tell 'em you're on the case...
...better yet, that you're close to cracking it...
...and they're gonna be all like, "Thank you, officer. How can we help?"
POLICE
$200.00
Talia, $200 is all I've got in the world right now.
If I buy this thing I won't be able to make rent this month.
Brody, the **reward money**.
You find the Penny Murderer and your days of paying rent will be over.

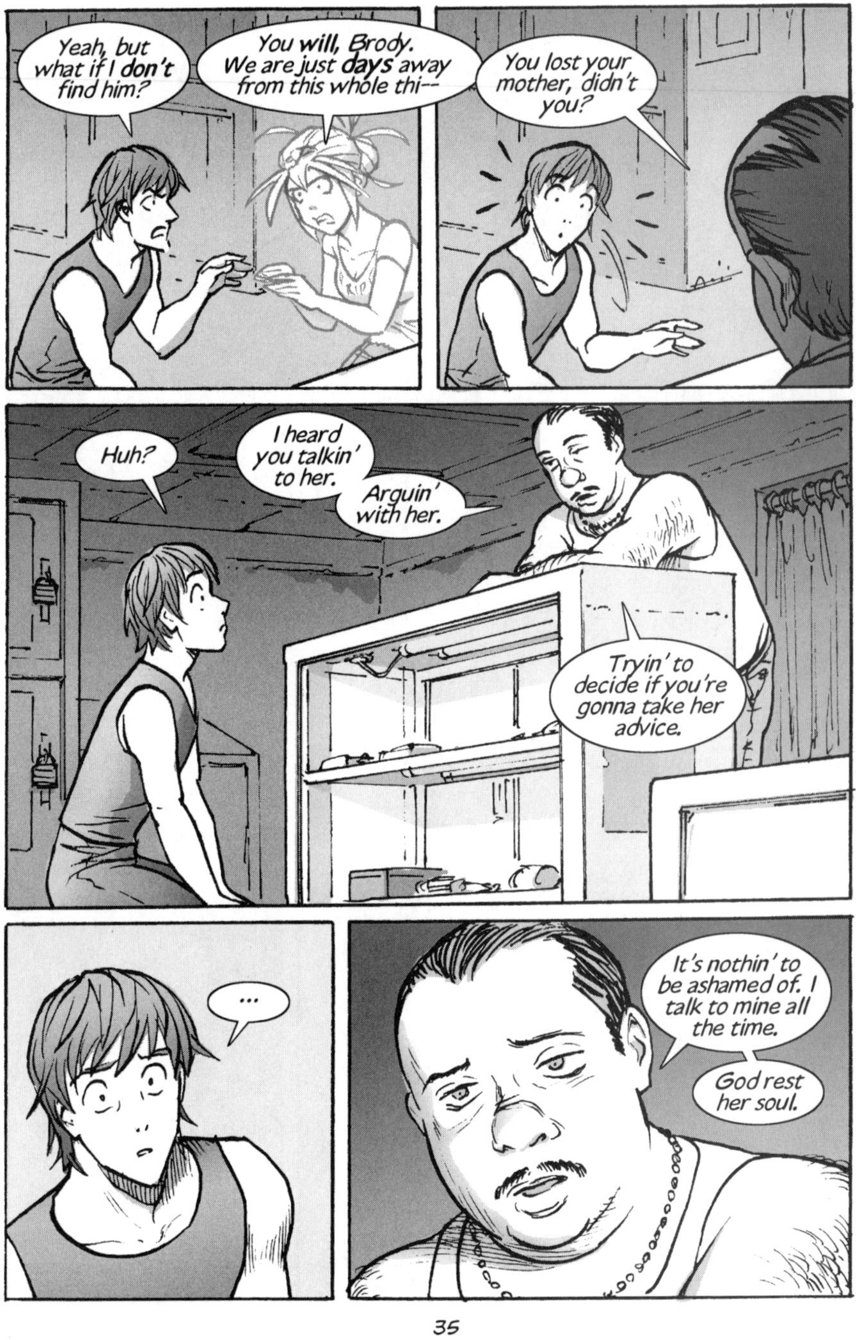
Yeah, but what if I **don't** find him?
You **will**, Brody. We are just **days** away from this whole thi--
You lost your mother, didn't you?
Huh?
I heard you talkin' to her.
Arguin' with her.
Tryin' to decide if you're gonna take her advice.
...
It's nothin' to be ashamed of. I talk to mine all the time.
God rest her soul.

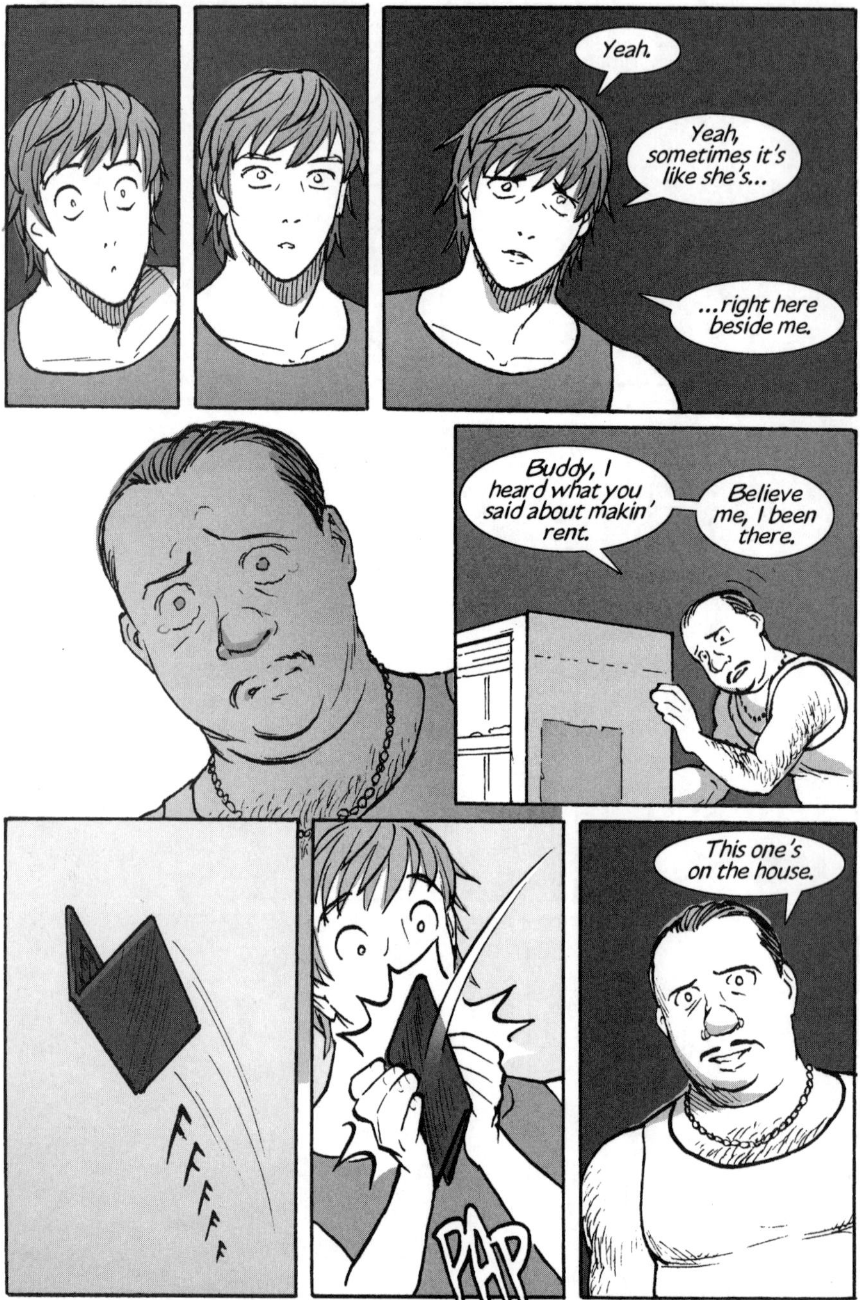
Yeah.
Yeah, sometimes it's like she's...
...right here beside me.
Buddy, I heard what you said about makin' rent.
Believe me, I been there.
FFFFF
PAP
This one's on the house.

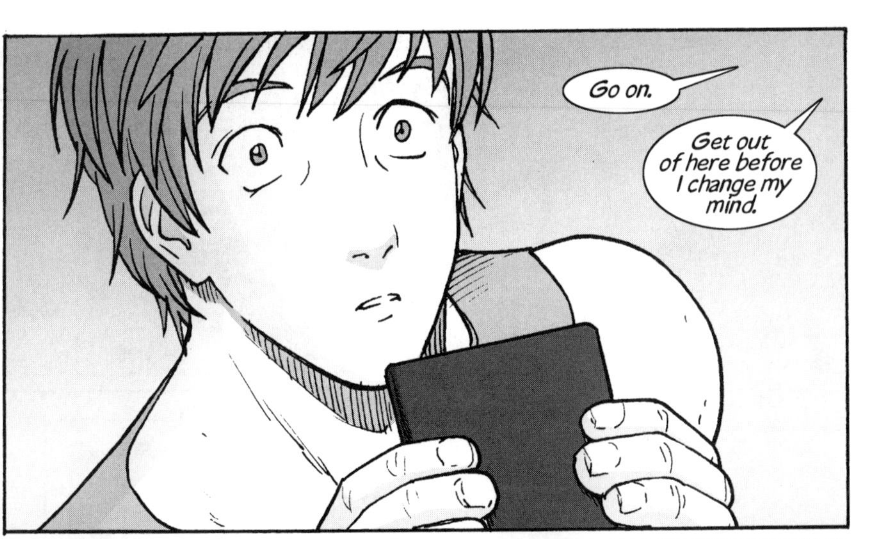
Go on.
Get out of here before I change my mind.

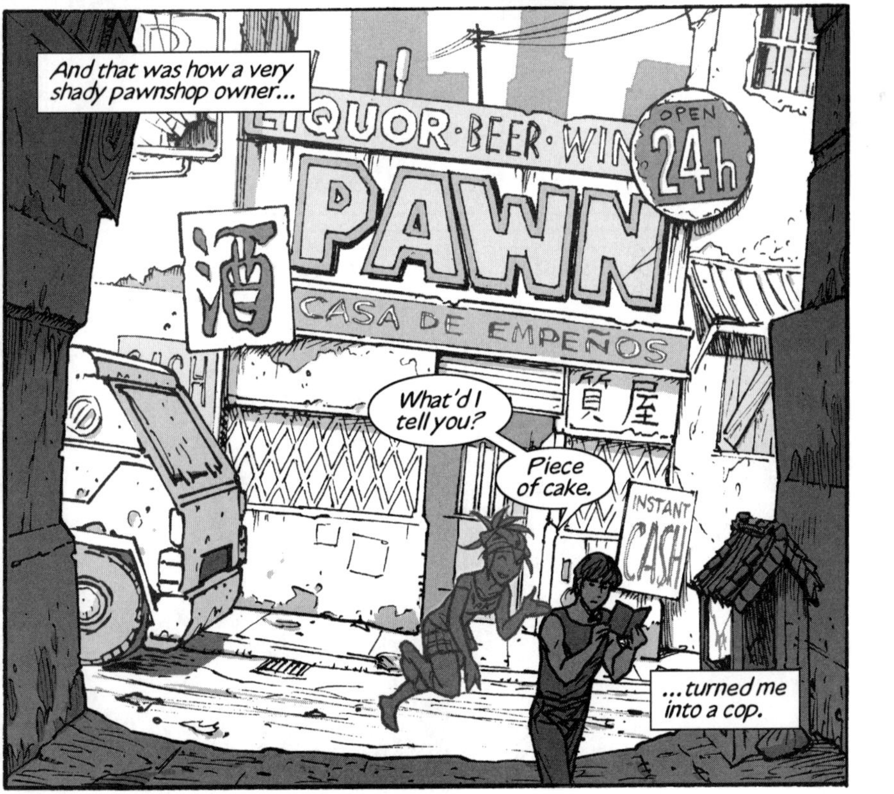
And that was how a very shady pawnshop owner...
LIQUOR·BEER·WIN
OPEN 24h
PAWN
CASA DE EMPEÑOS
What'd I tell you?
Piece of cake.
INSTANT CASH
...turned me into a cop.

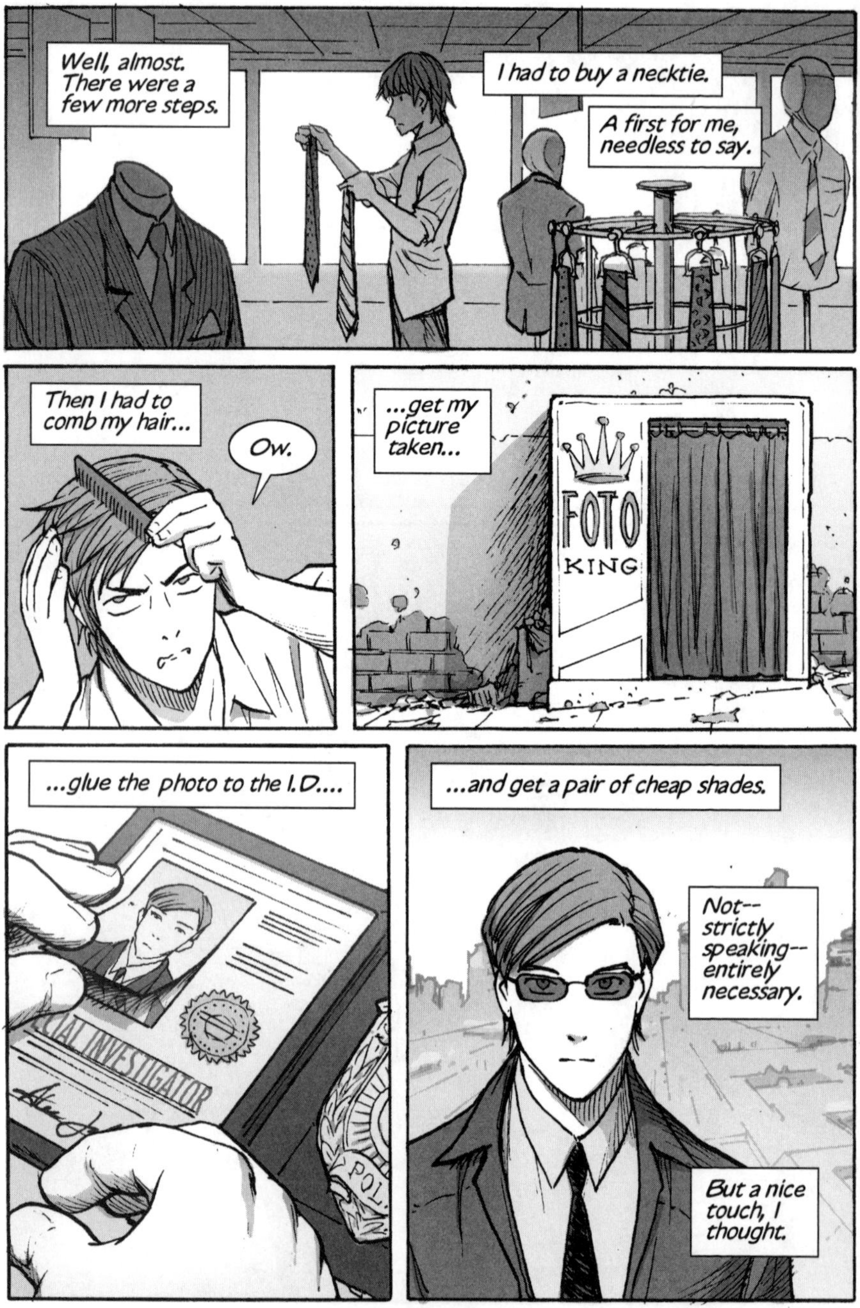
Well, almost. There were a few more steps.
I had to buy a necktie.
A first for me, needless to say.
Then I had to comb my hair...
Ow.
...get my picture taken...
FOTO KING
...glue the photo to the I.D....
...and get a pair of cheap shades.
Not-- strictly speaking-- entirely necessary.
But a nice touch, I thought.

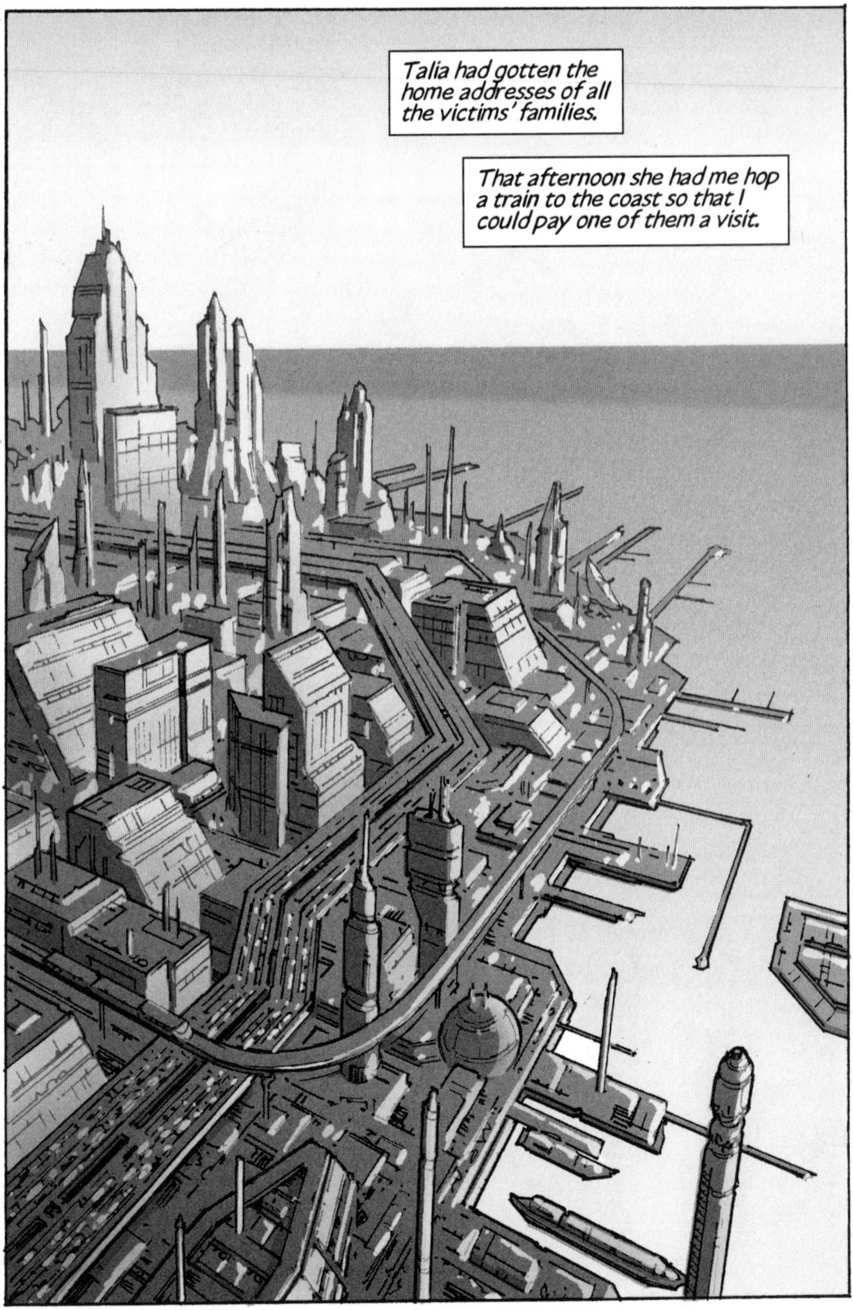
Talia had gotten the home addresses of all the victims' families.
That afternoon she had me hop a train to the coast so that I could pay one of them a visit.

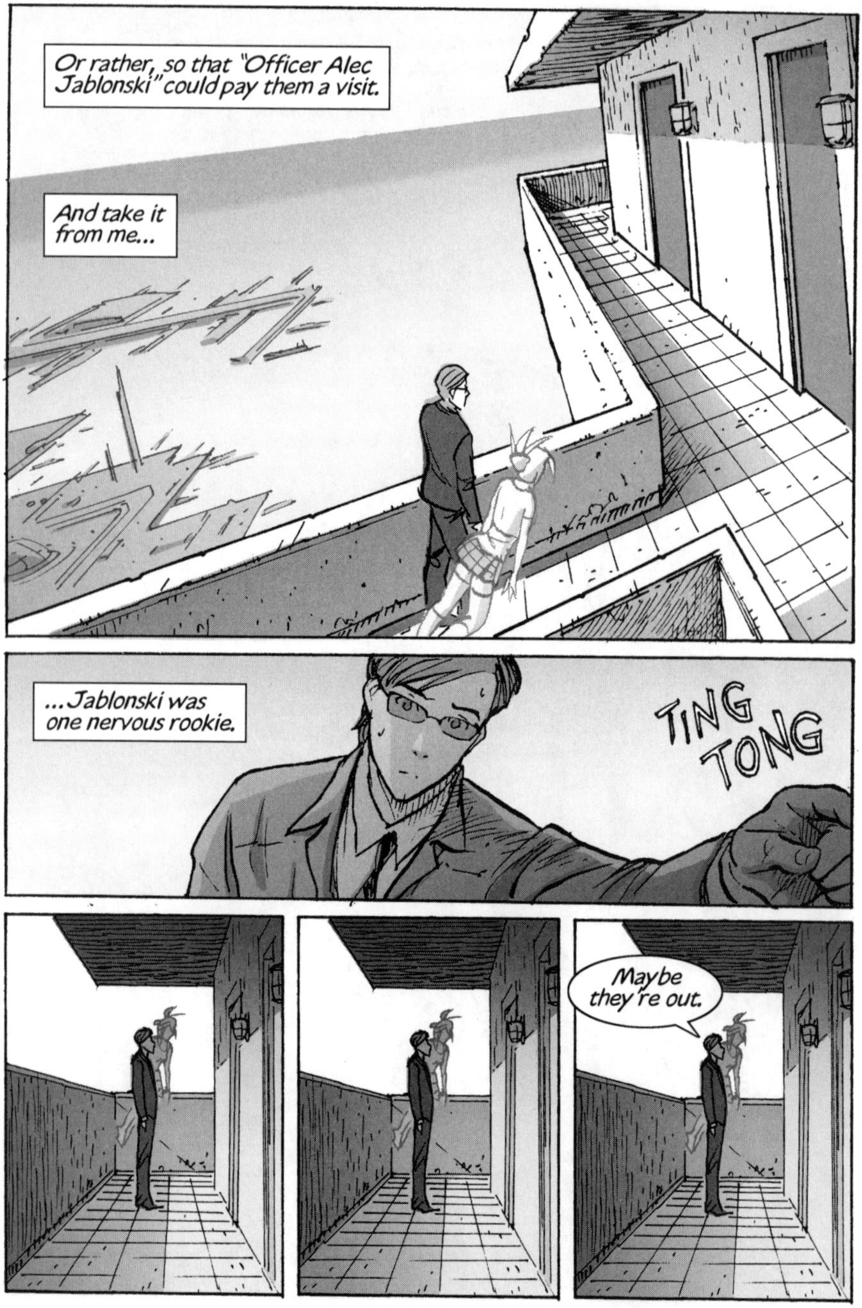

Or rather, so that "Officer Alec Jablonski" could pay them a visit.
And take it from me...
...Jablonski was one nervous rookie.
TING TONG
Maybe they're out.

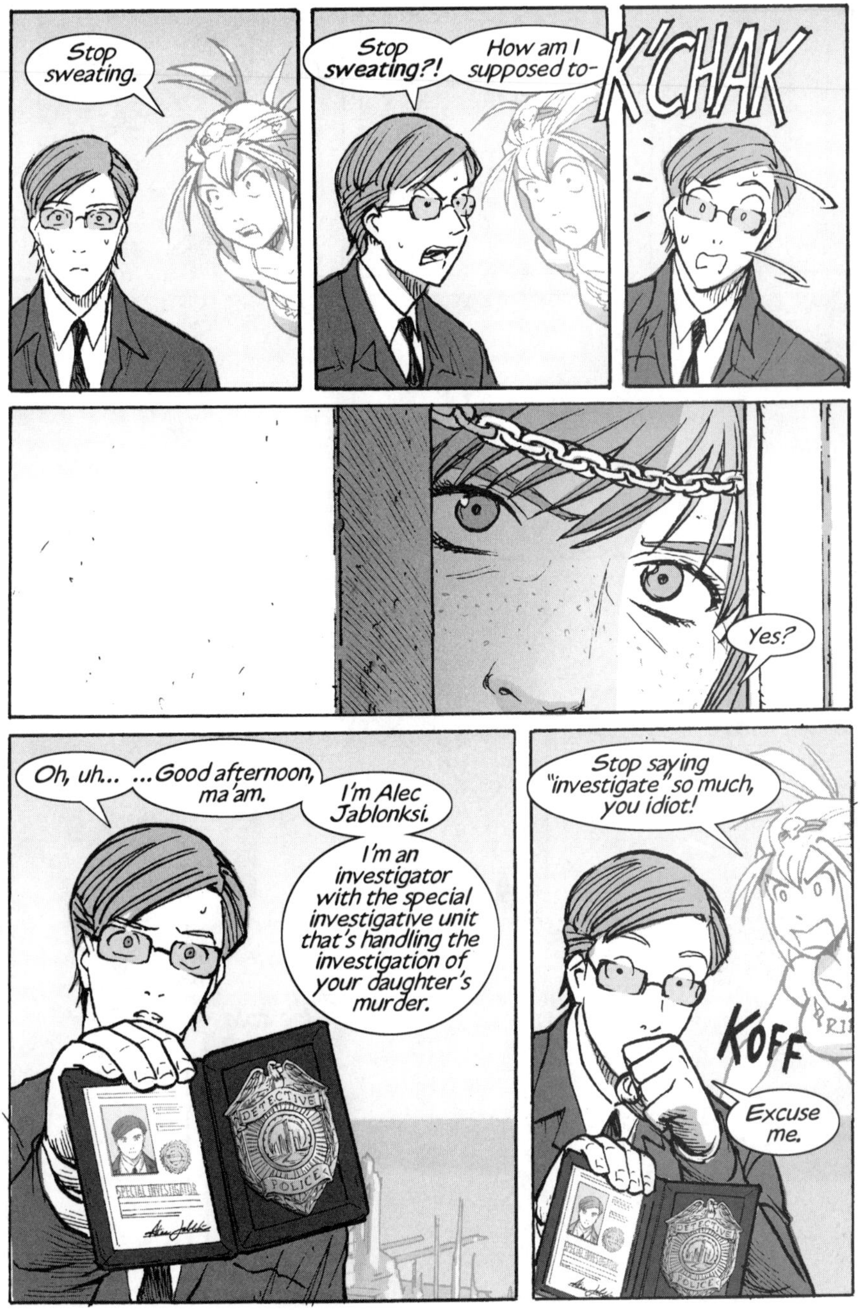
Stop sweating.
Stop sweating?!
How am I supposed to-
K'CHAK
Yes?
Oh, uh...
...Good afternoon, ma'am.
I'm Alec Jablonksi.
I'm an investigator with the special investigative unit that's handling the investigation of your daughter's murder.
DETECTIVE
POLICE
SPECIAL INVESTIGATOR
Stop saying "investigate" so much, you idiot!
KOFF
Excuse me.

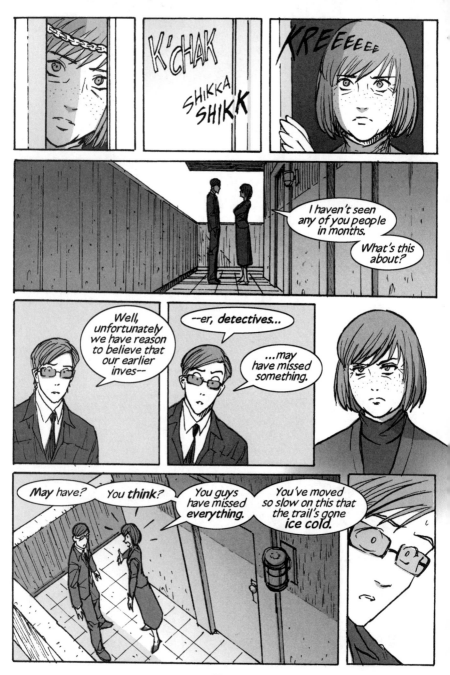

K'CHAK

SHIKKA
SHIKK

KREEEEEE

I haven't seen any of you people in months.

What's this about?

Well, unfortunately we have reason to believe that our earlier inves--

--er, detectives...

...may have missed something.

May have?

You think?

You guys have missed everything.

You've moved so slow on this that the trail's gone ice cold.

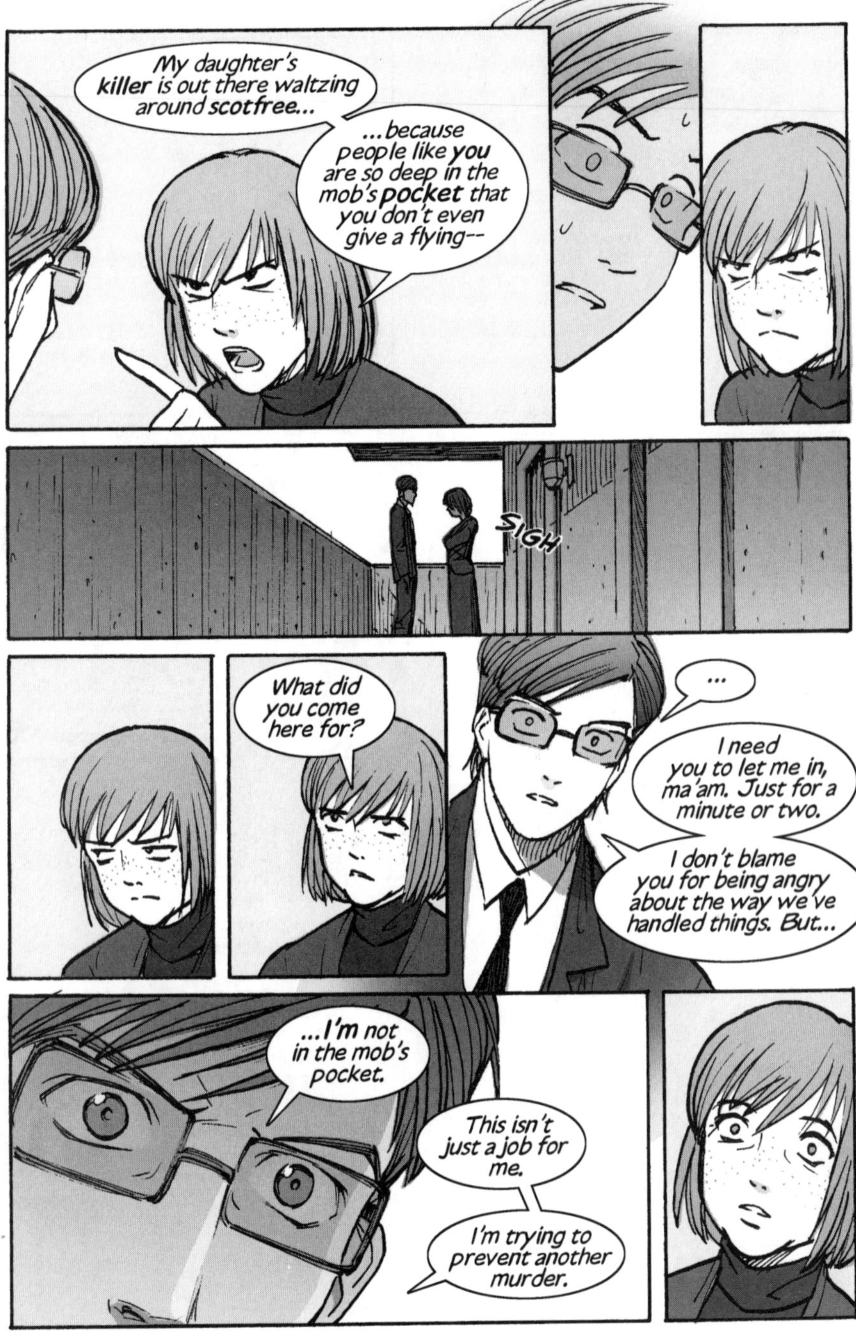
My daughter's killer is out there waltzing around scotfree...
...because people like you are so deep in the mob's pocket that you don't even give a flying--
SIGH
What did you come here for?
...
I need you to let me in, ma'am. Just for a minute or two.
I don't blame you for being angry about the way we've handled things. But...
...I'm not in the mob's pocket.
This isn't just a job for me.
I'm trying to prevent another murder.

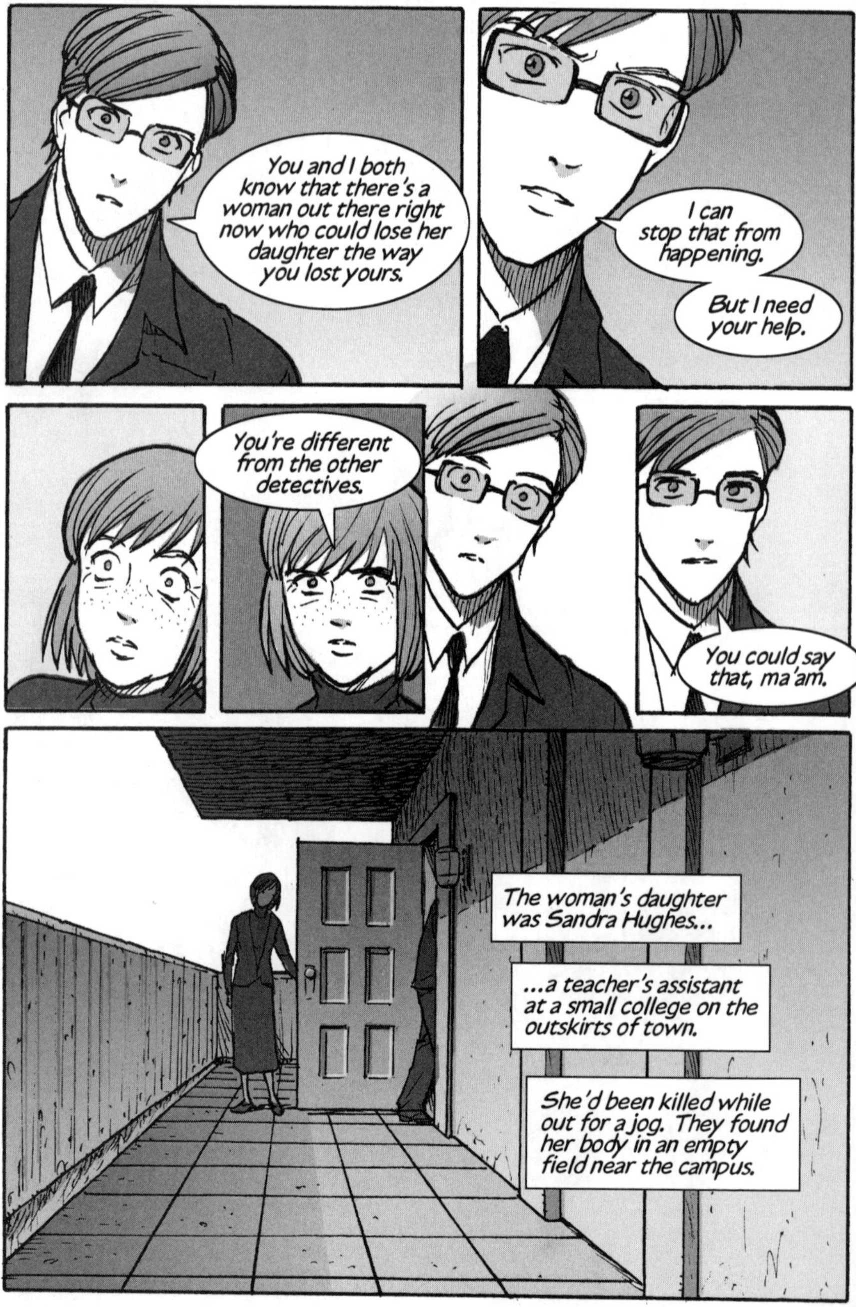
You and I both know that there's a woman out there right now who could lose her daughter the way you lost yours.
I can stop that from happening.
But I need your help.
You're different from the other detectives.
You could say that, ma'am.
The woman's daughter was Sandra Hughes...
...a teacher's assistant at a small college on the outskirts of town.
She'd been killed while out for a jog. They found her body in an empty field near the campus.

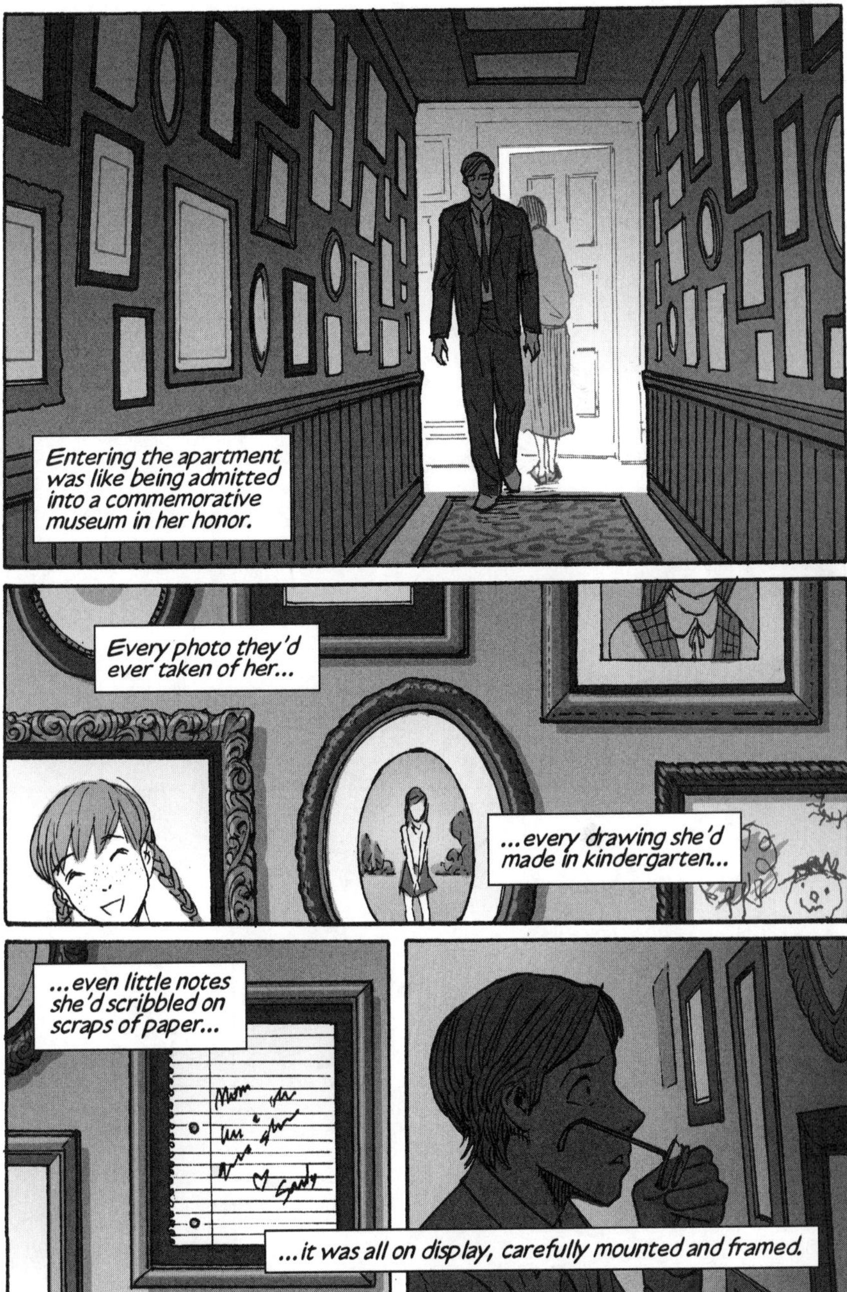
Entering the apartment was like being admitted into a commemorative museum in her honor.
Every photo they'd ever taken of her...
...every drawing she'd made in kindergarten...
...even little notes she'd scribbled on scraps of paper...
...it was all on display, carefully mounted and framed.

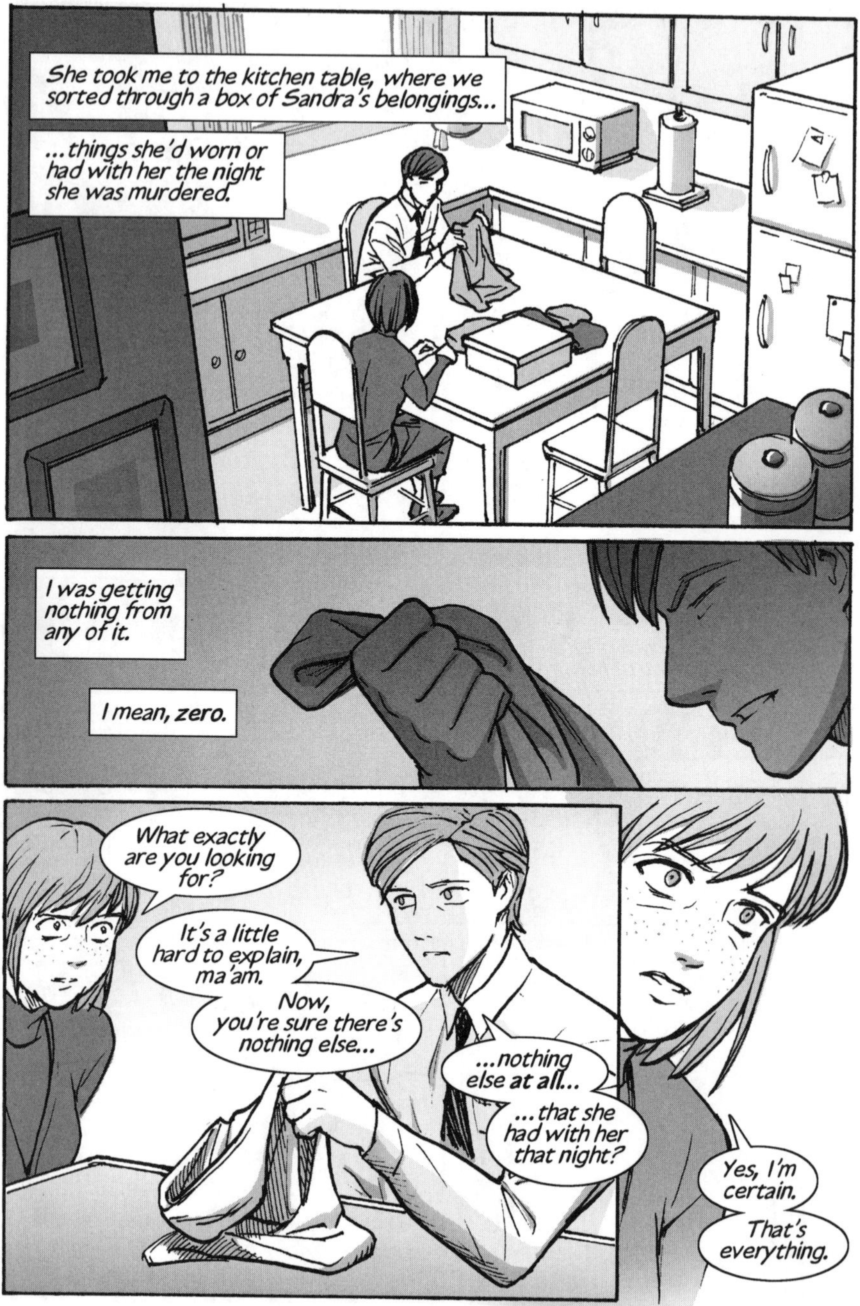
She took me to the kitchen table, where we sorted through a box of Sandra's belongings...
...things she'd worn or had with her the night she was murdered.
I was getting nothing from any of it.
I mean, zero.
What exactly are you looking for?
It's a little hard to explain, ma'am.
Now, you're sure there's nothing else...
...nothing else at all...
...that she had with her that night?
Yes, I'm certain.
That's everything.

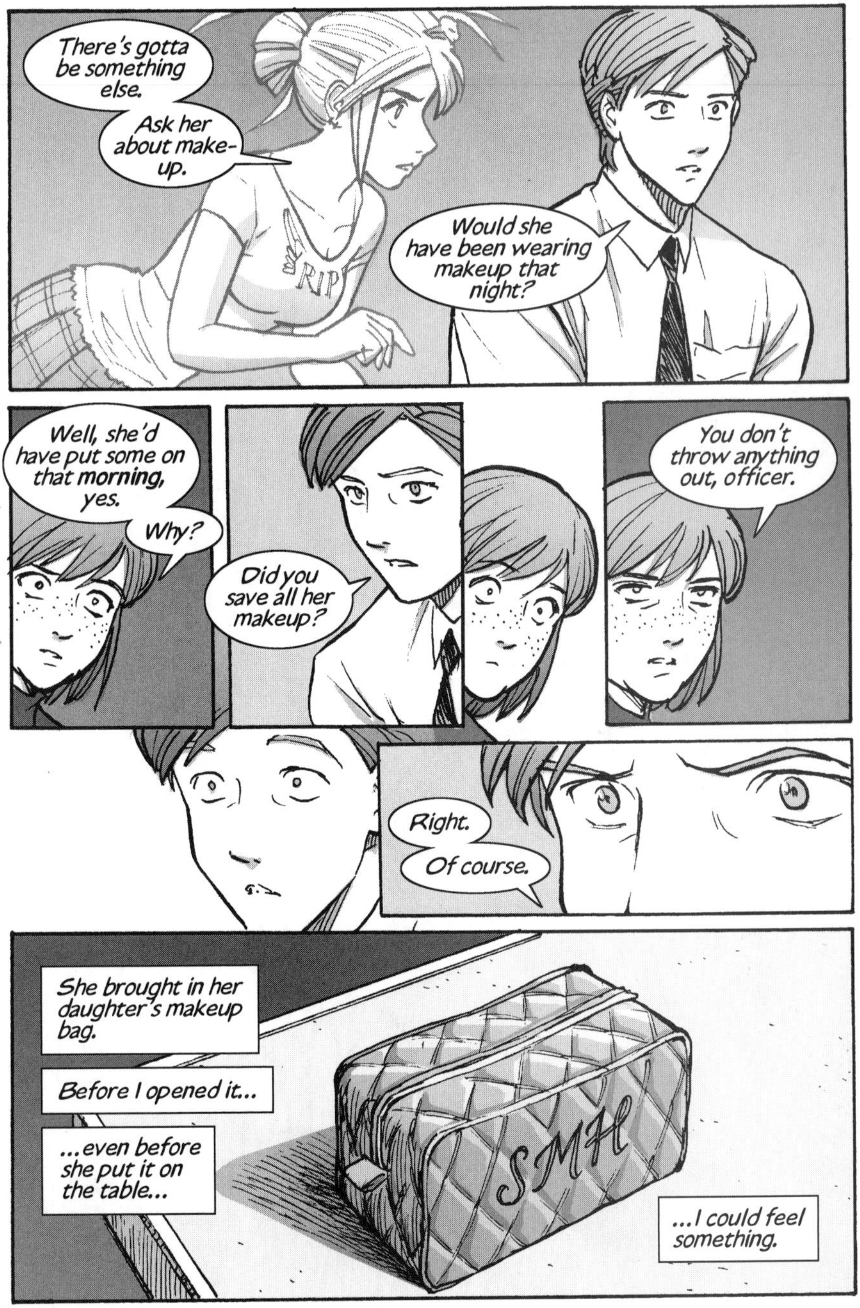
There's gotta be something else.
Ask her about make-up.
Would she have been wearing makeup that night?
Well, she'd have put some on that **morning**, yes.
Why?
Did you save all her makeup?
You don't throw anything out, officer.
Right.
Of course.
She brought in her daughter's makeup bag.
Before I opened it...
...even before she put it on the table...
SMH
...I could feel something.

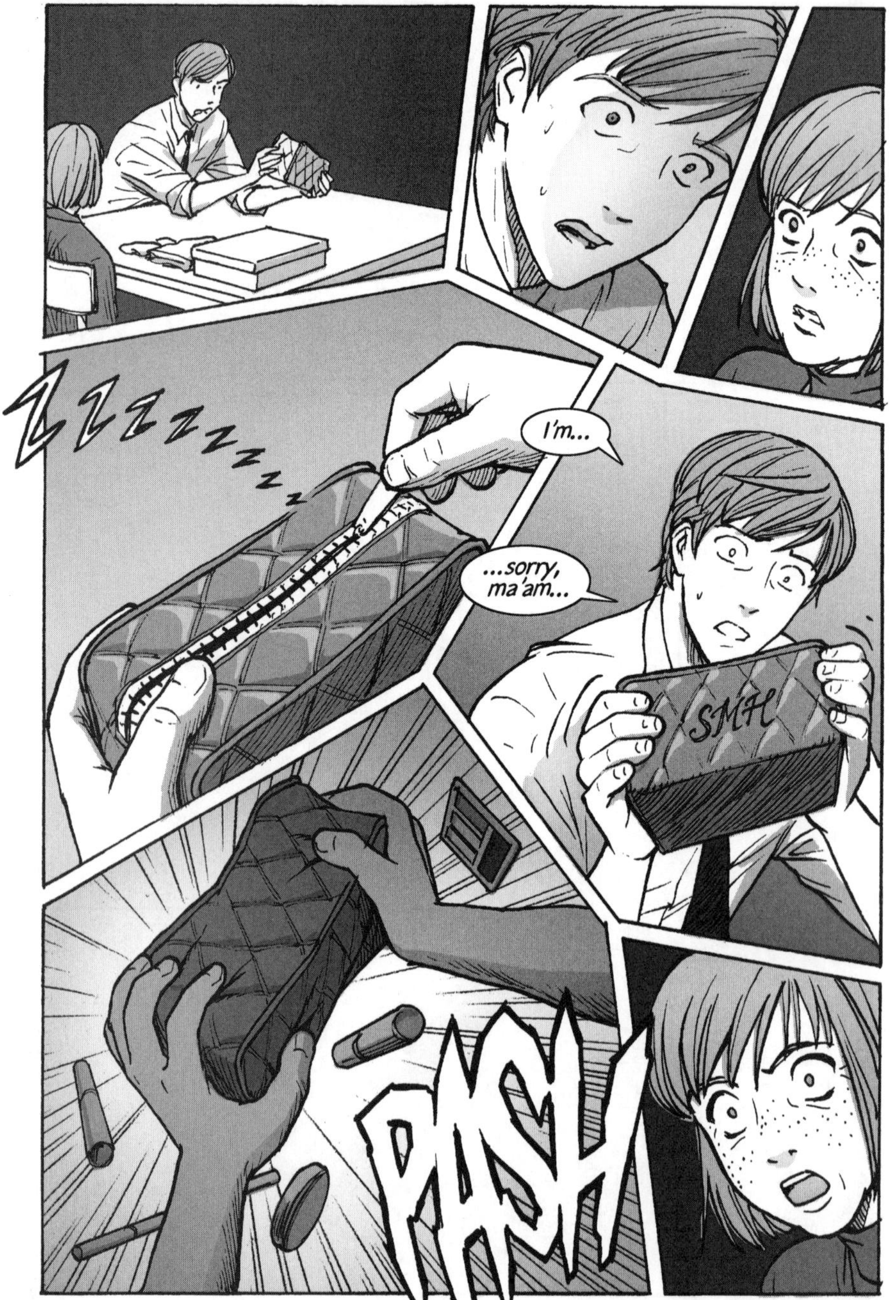
ZZZZZZZZZZZ
I'm...
...sorry, ma'am...
SMH
PASH

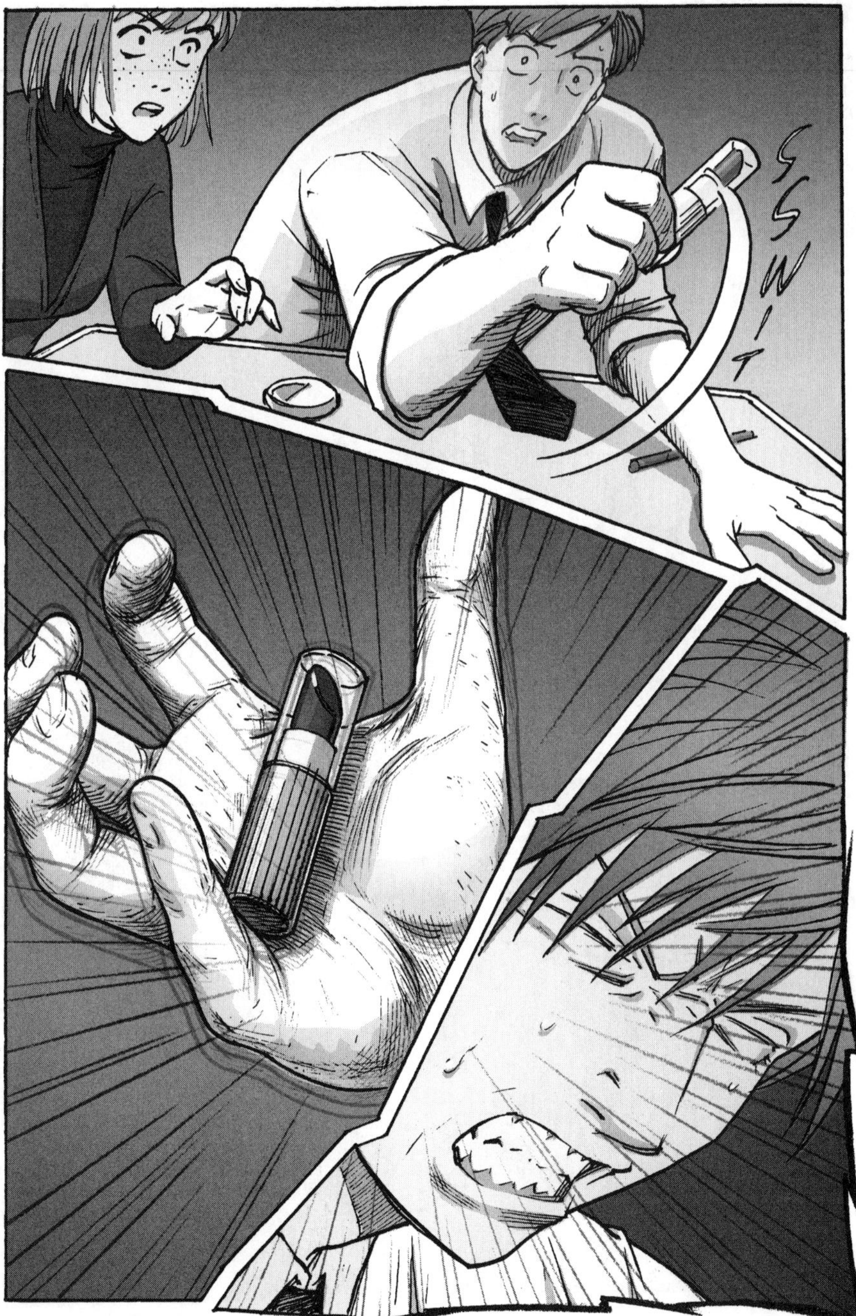
SSWIT

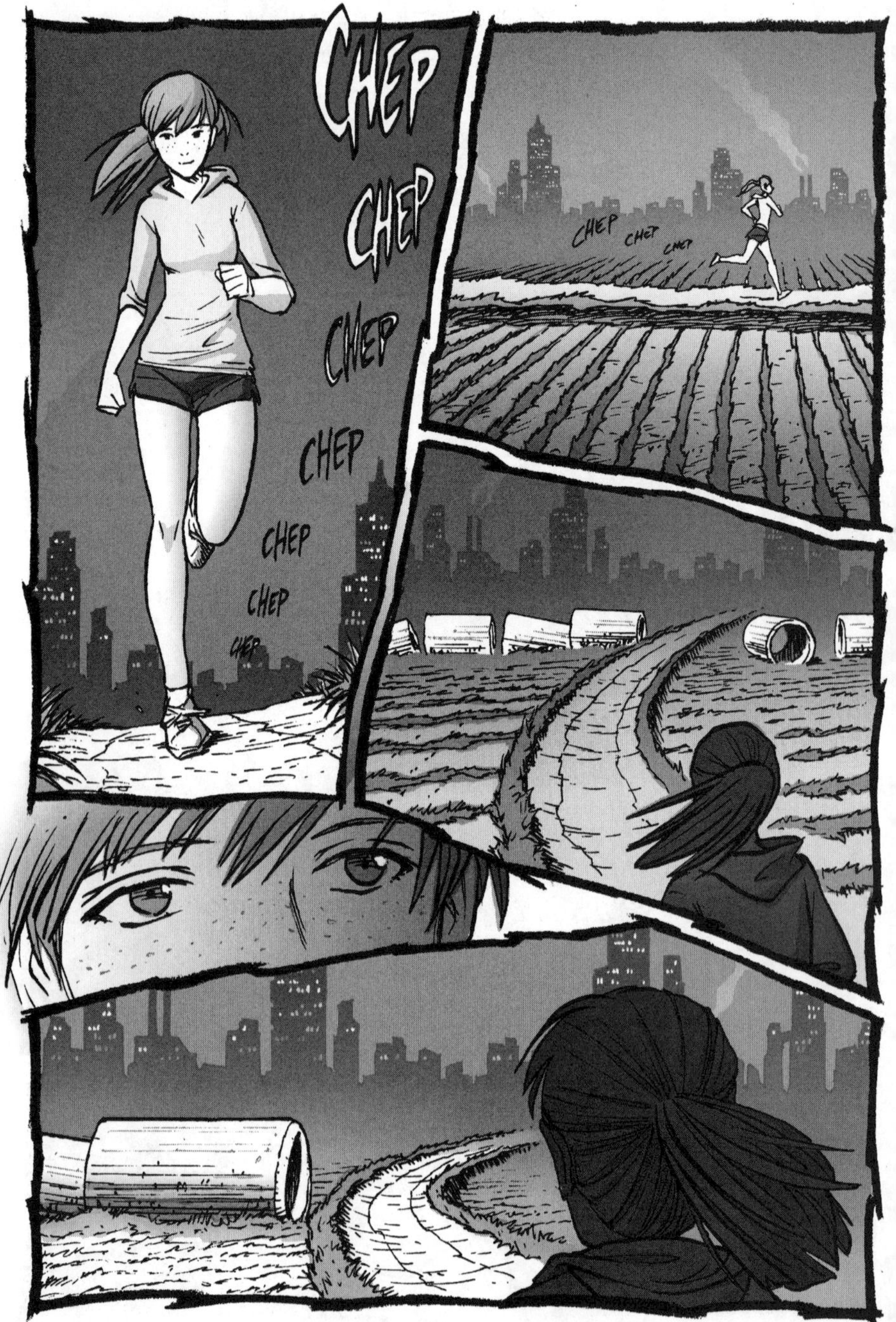
CHEP
CHEP
CHEP
CHEP
CHEP
CHEP
CHEP
CHEP
CHEP
CHEP

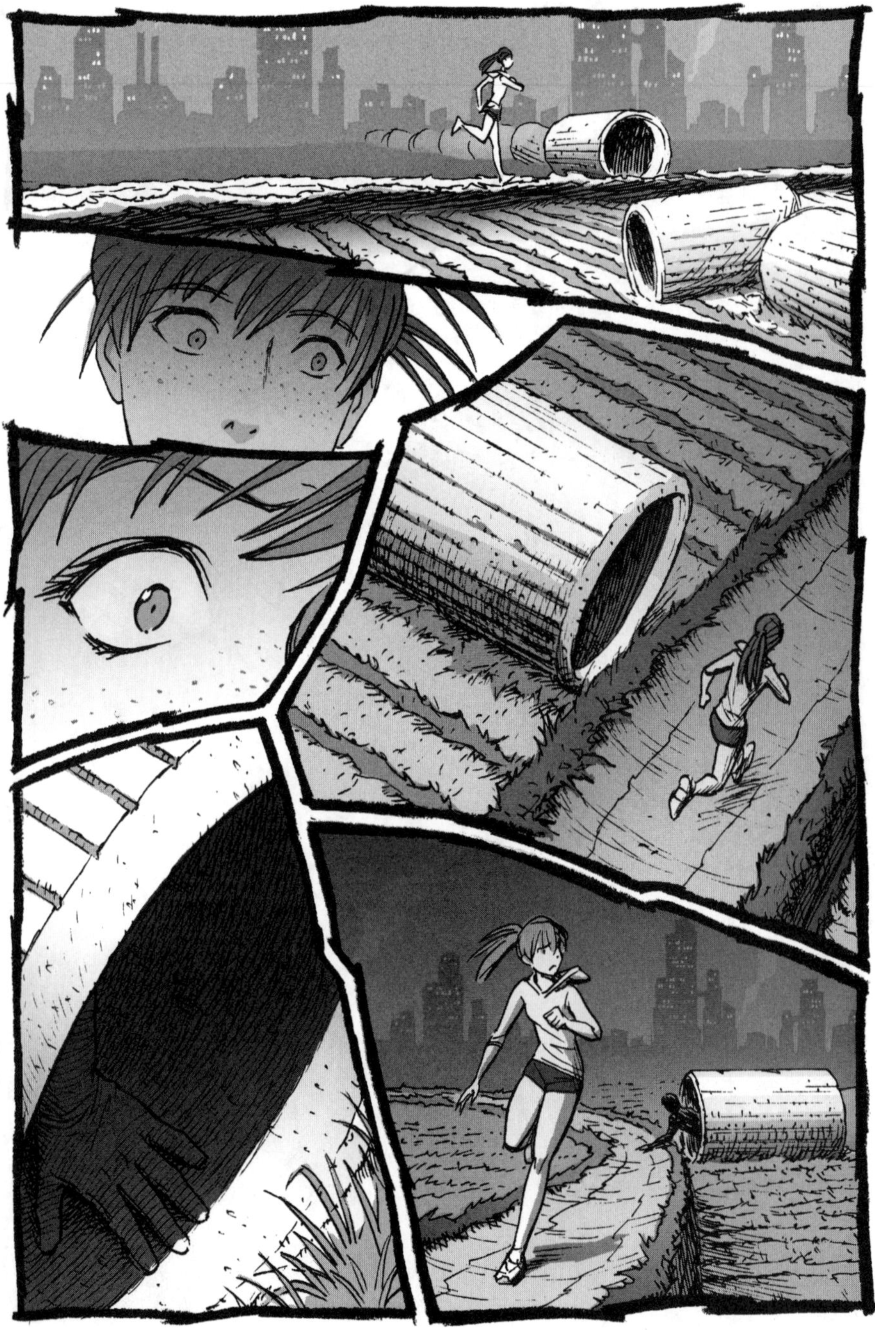

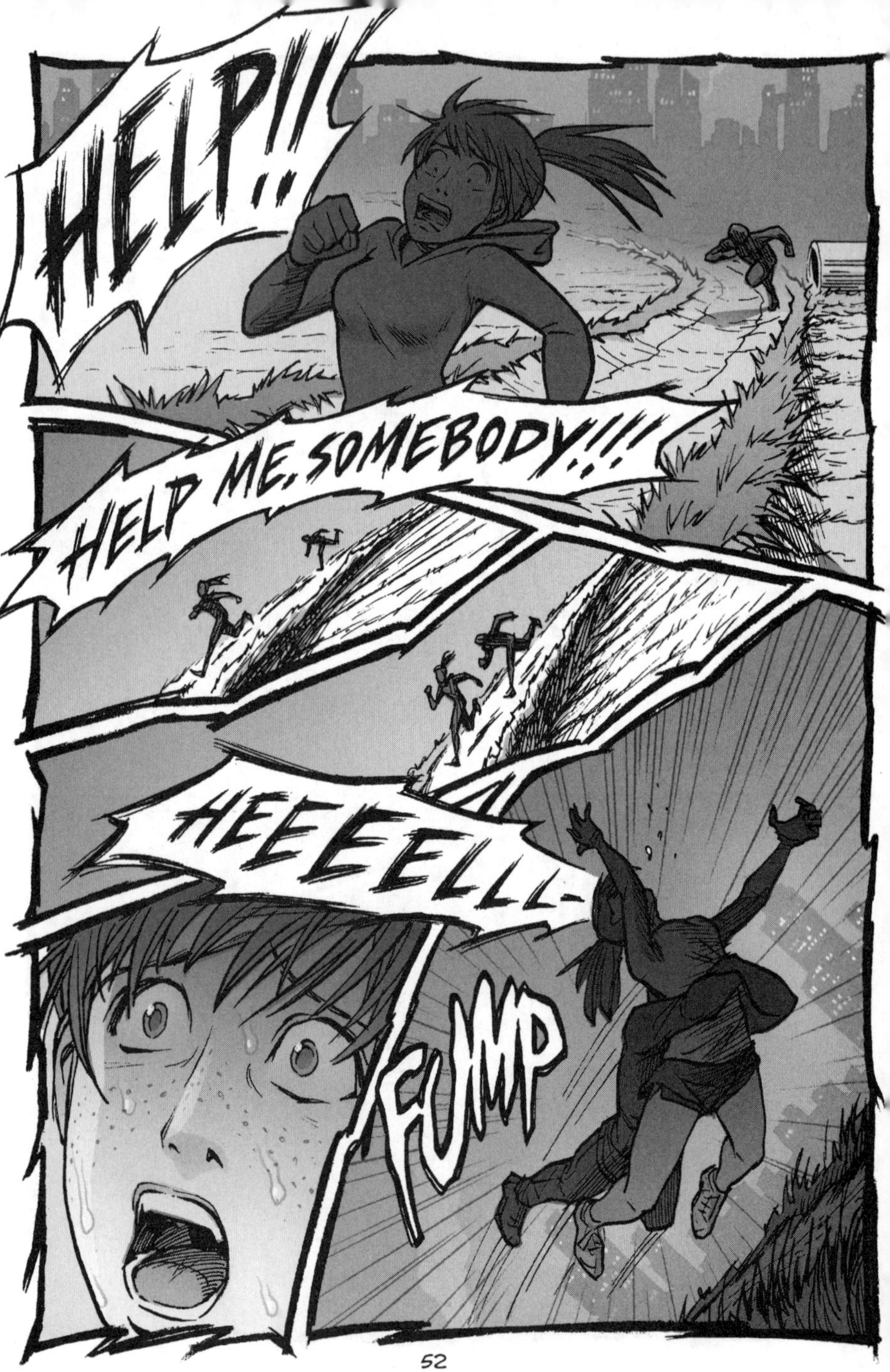
HELP!!
HELP ME, SOMEBODY!!!
HEEEELLL-
FUMP

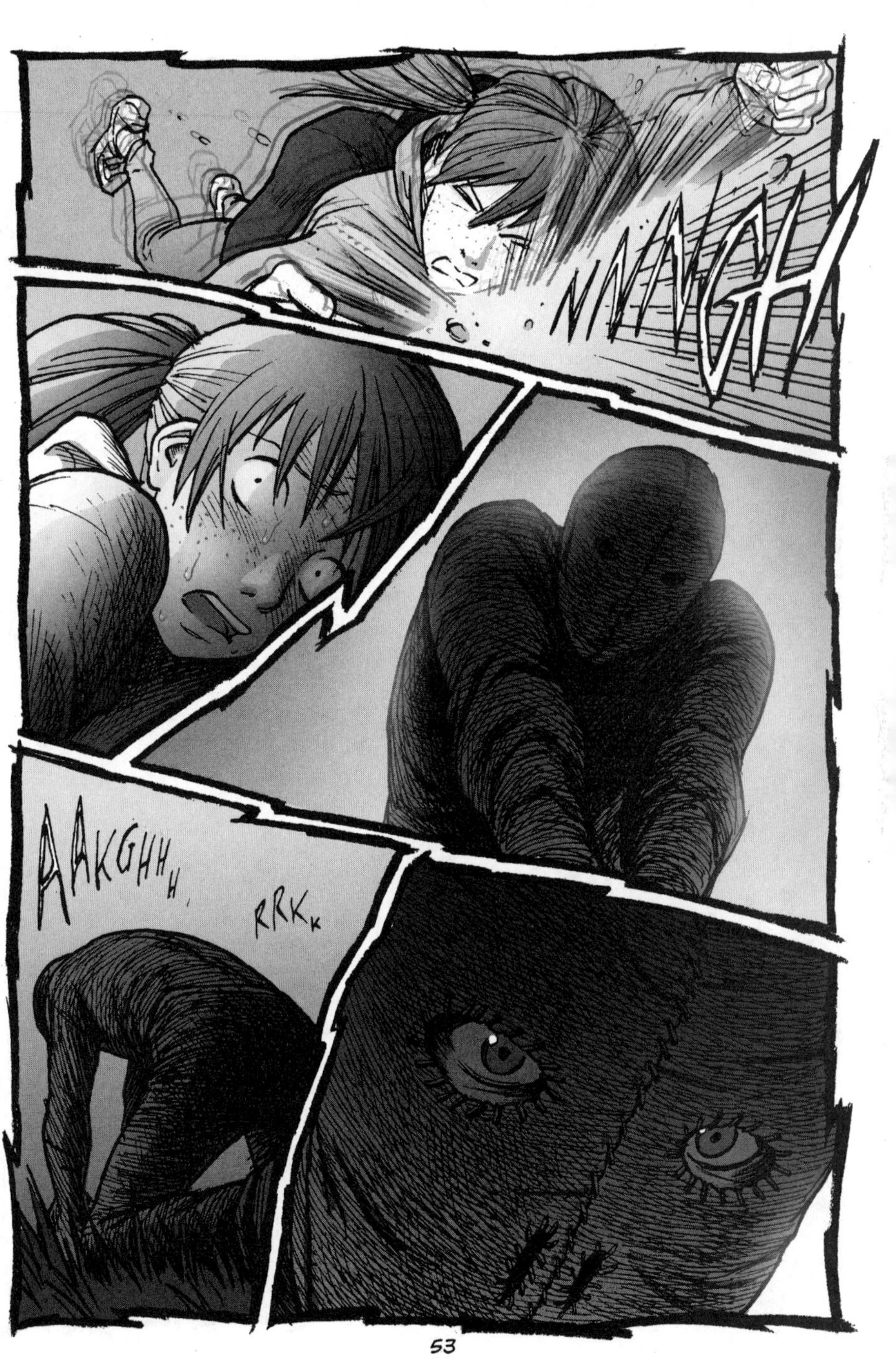
NNNGAH
AAKGHHh
RRKk

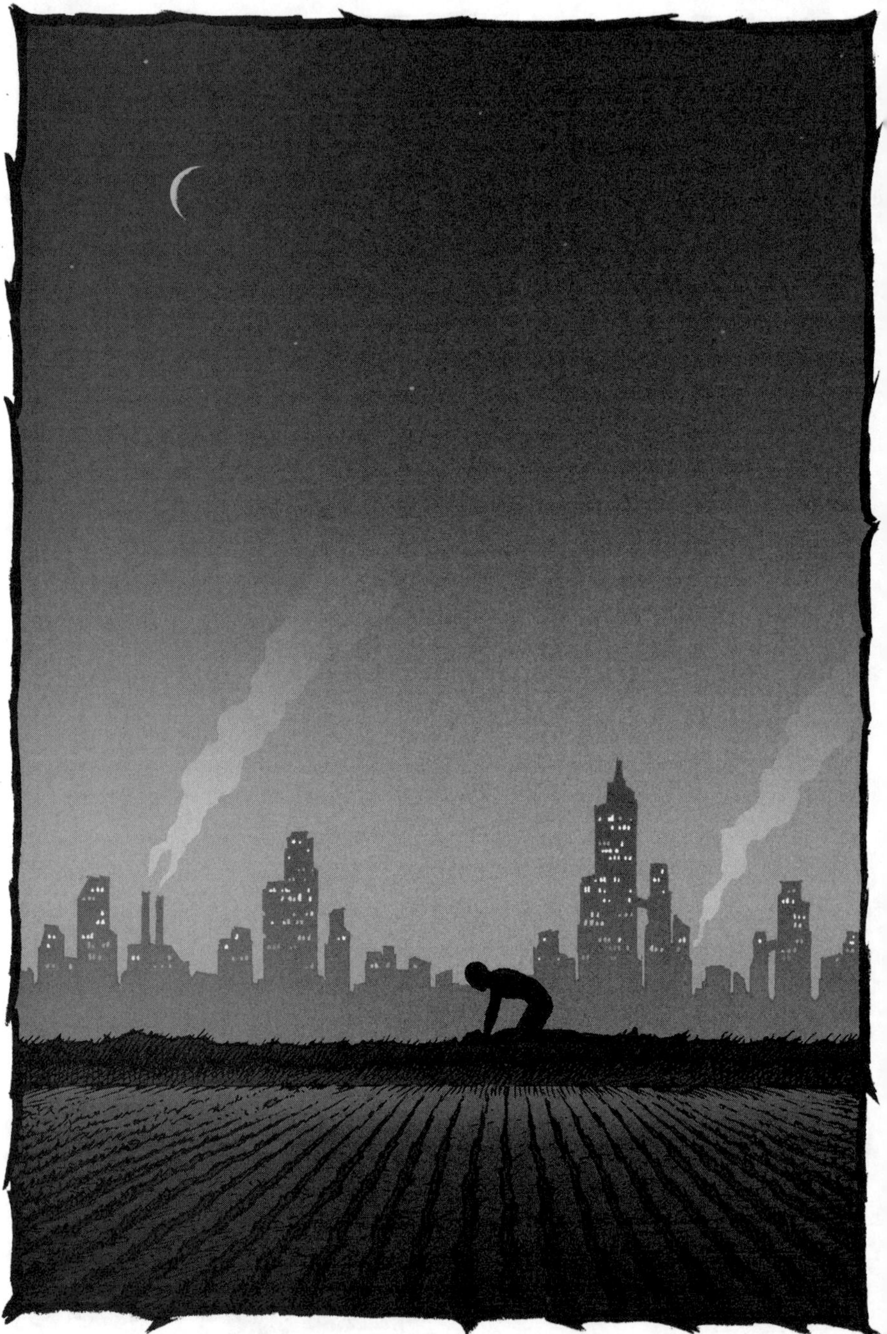

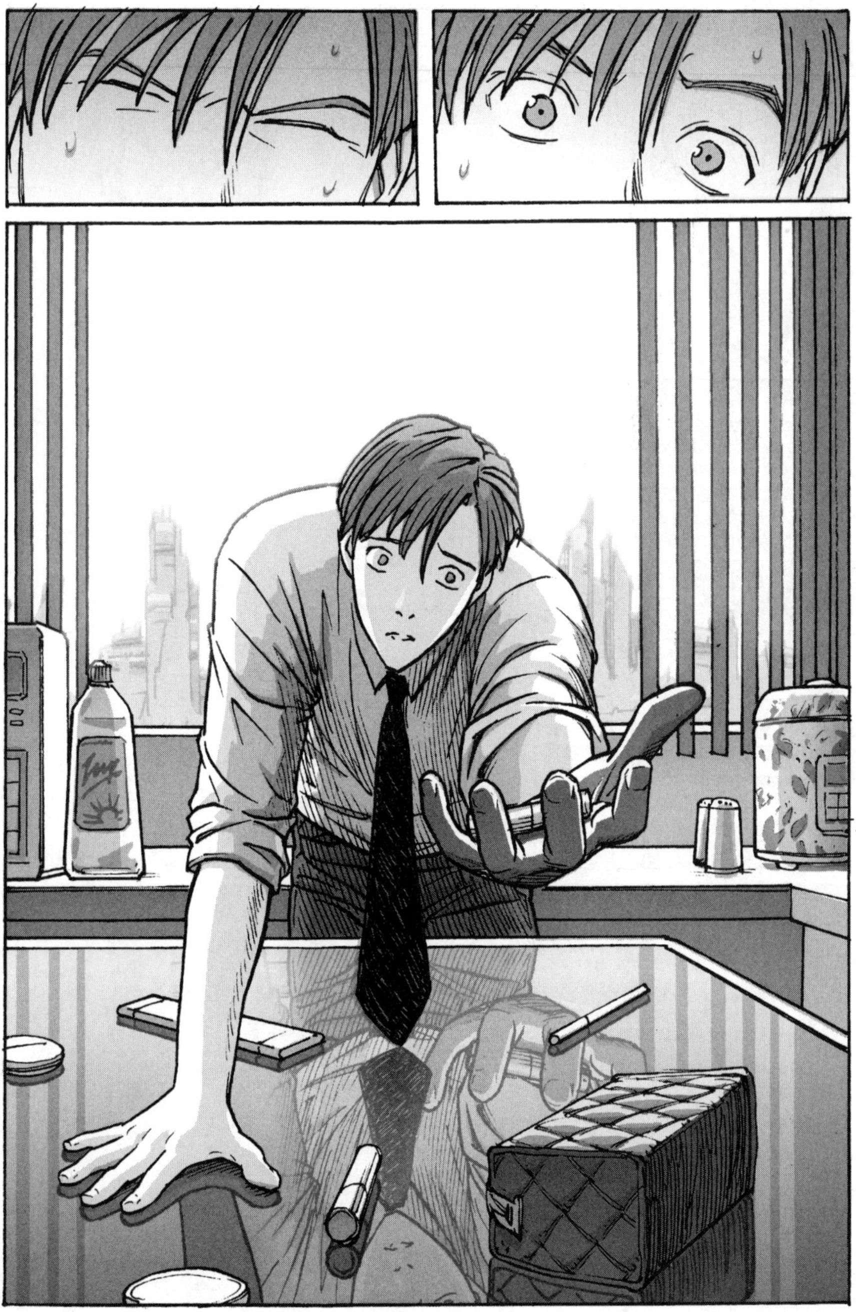

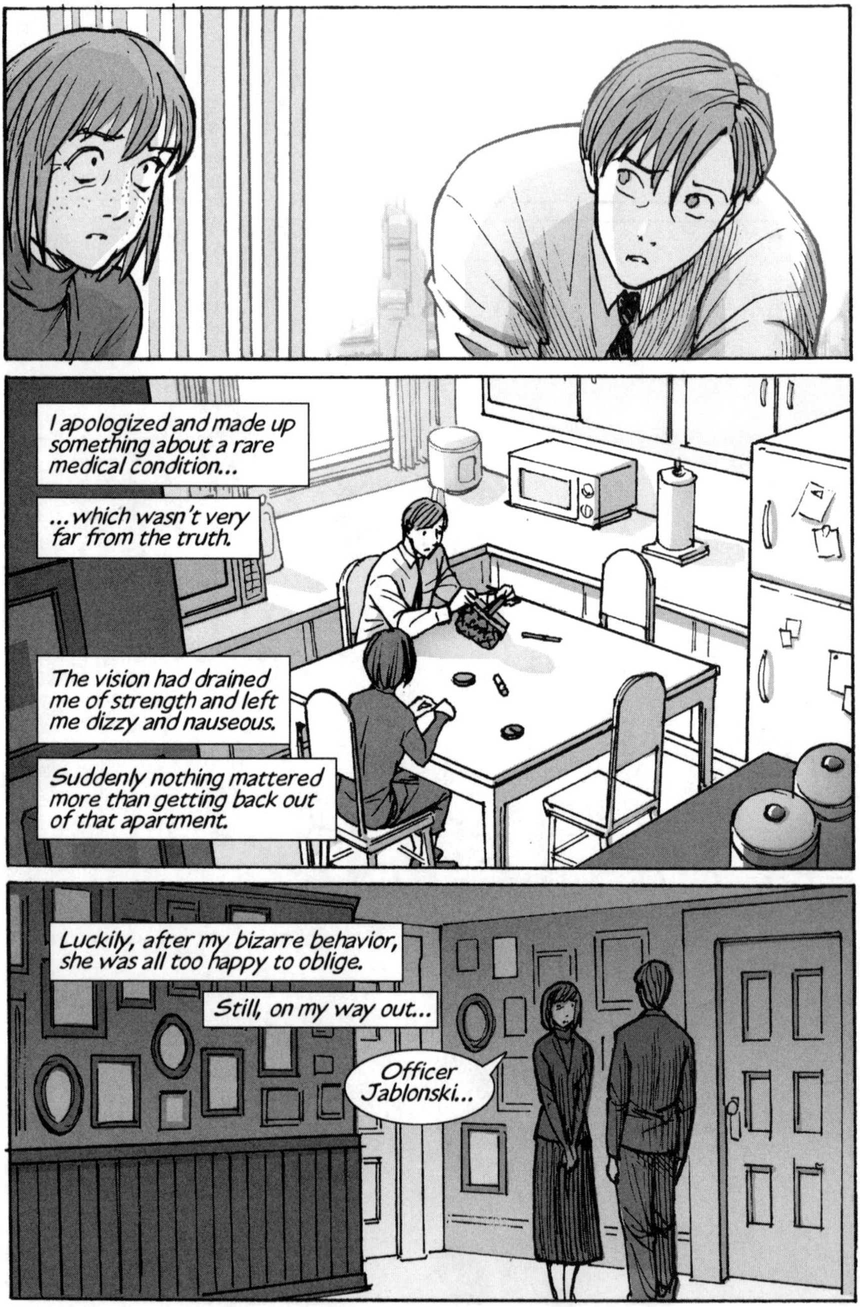
I apologized and made up something about a rare medical condition...
...which wasn't very far from the truth.
The vision had drained me of strength and left me dizzy and nauseous.
Suddenly nothing mattered more than getting back out of that apartment.
Luckily, after my bizarre behavior, she was all too happy to oblige.
Still, on my way out...
Officer Jablonski...

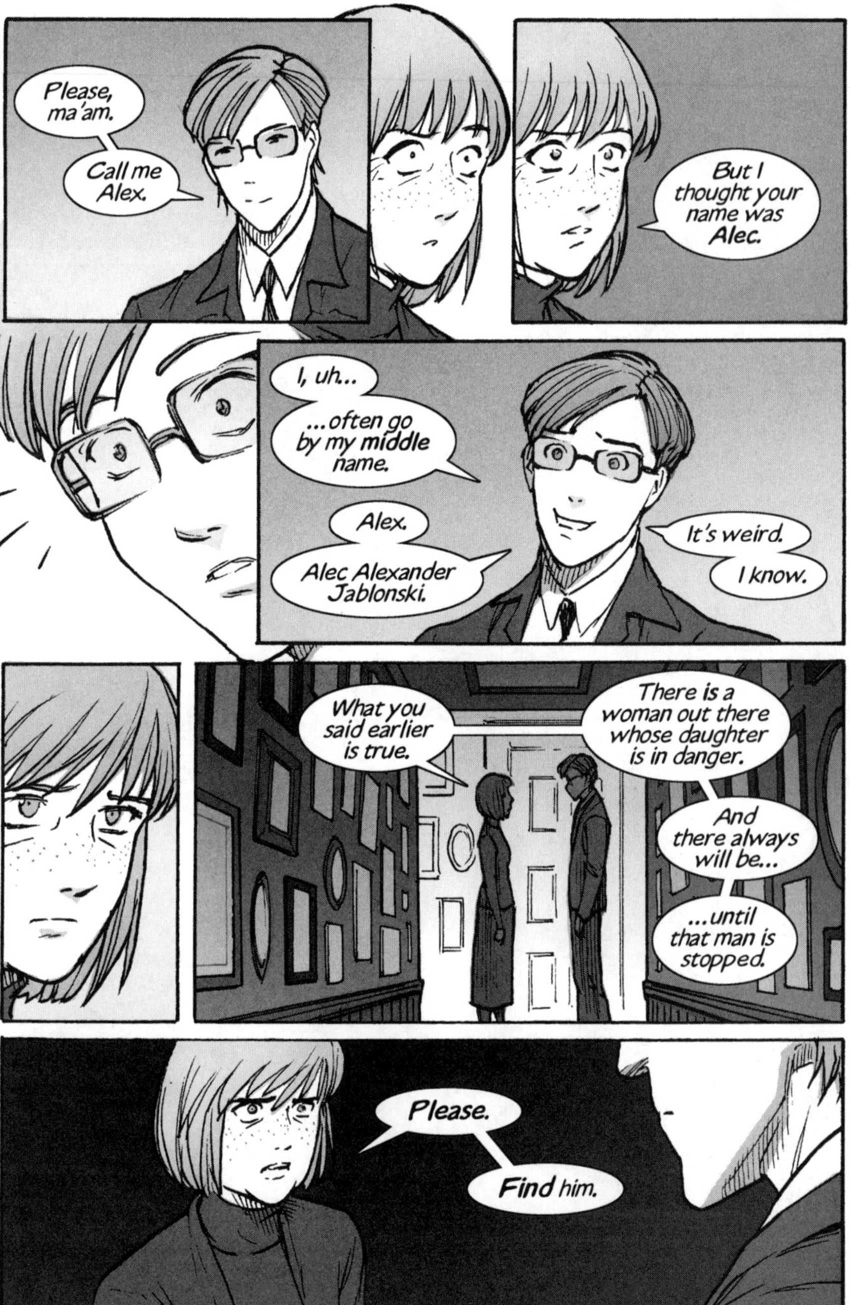
Please, ma'am.
Call me Alex.
But I thought your name was Alec.
I, uh...
...often go by my middle name.
Alex.
Alec Alexander Jablonski.
It's weird.
I know.
What you said earlier is true.
There is a woman out there whose daughter is in danger.
And there always will be...
...until that man is stopped.
Please.
Find him.

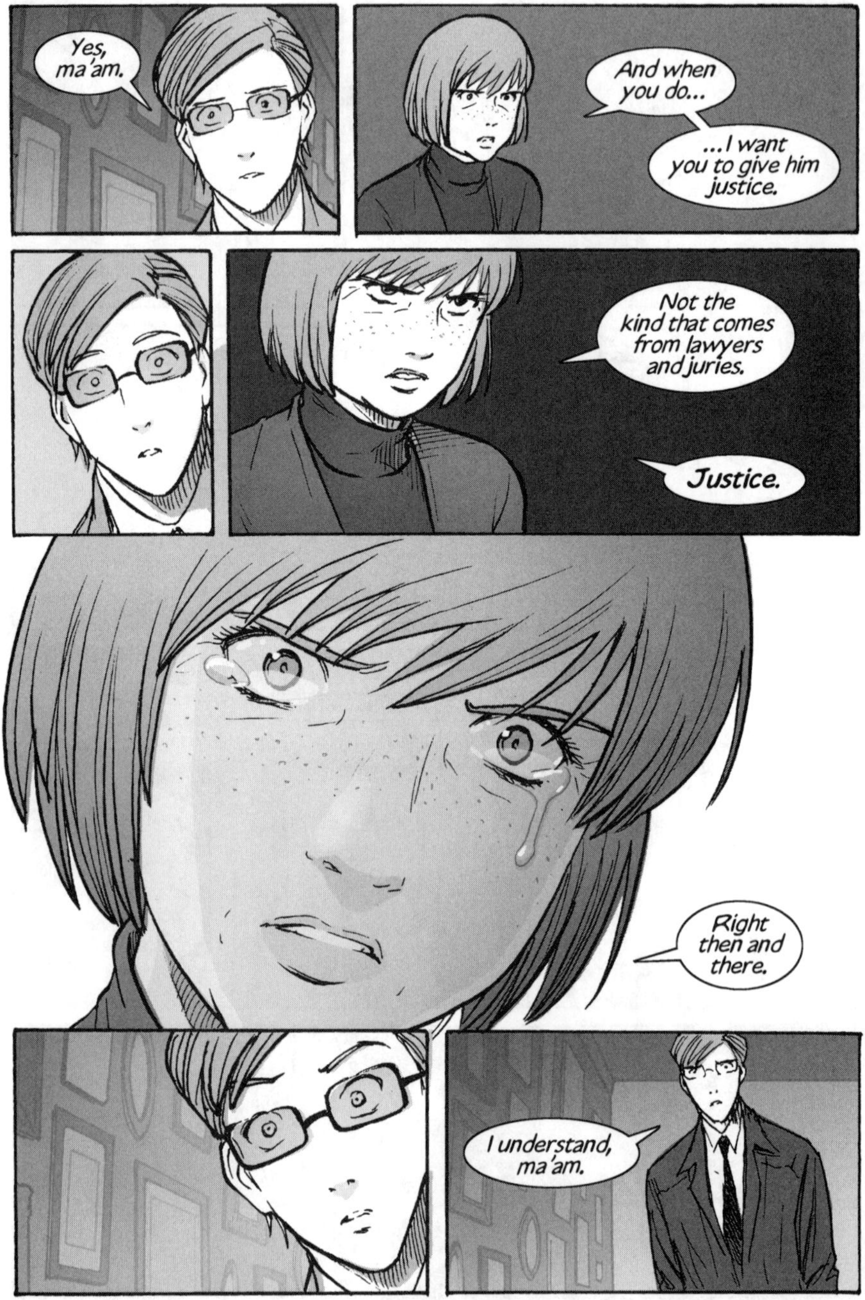

Yes, ma'am.
And when you do...
...I want you to give him justice.
Not the kind that comes from lawyers and juries.
Justice.
Right then and there.
I understand, ma'am.

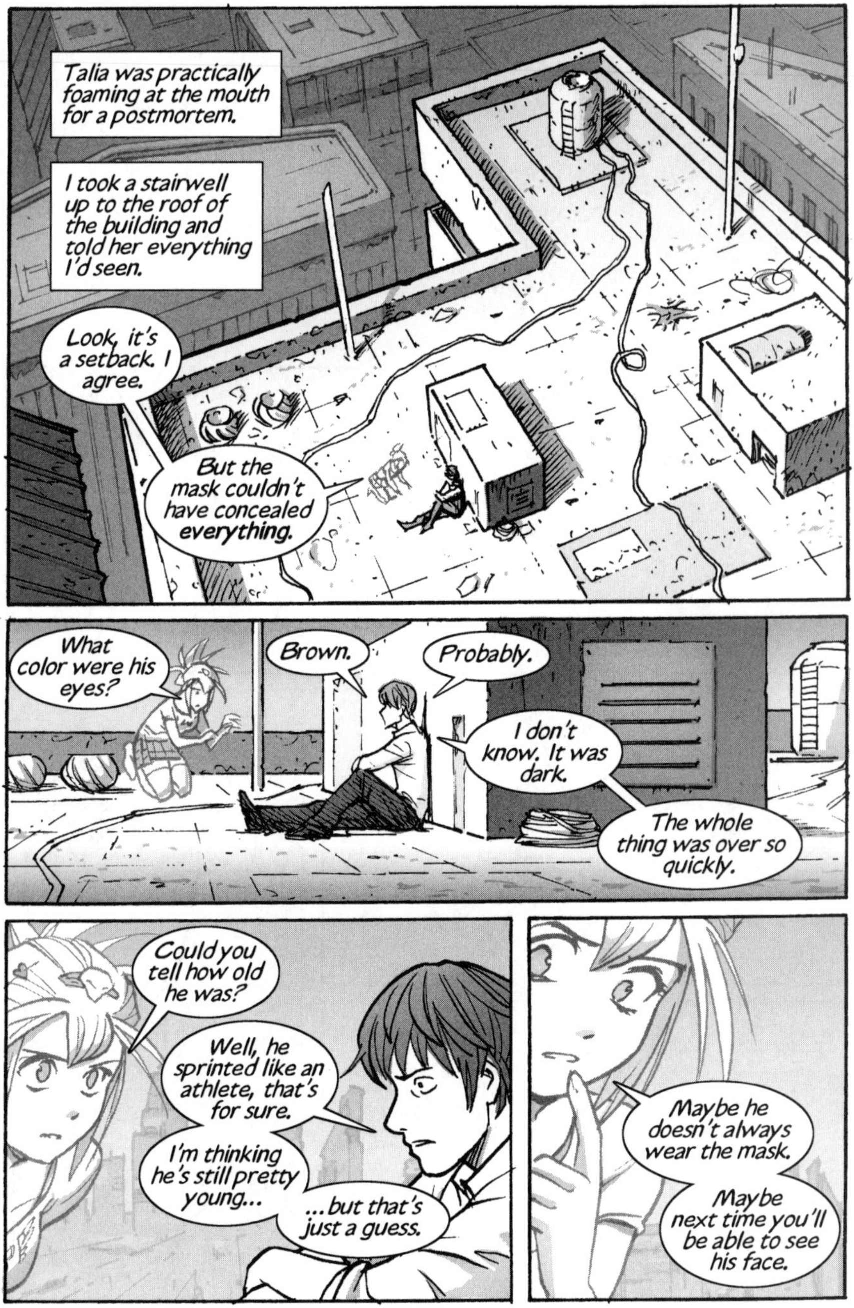
Talia was practically foaming at the mouth for a postmortem.
I took a stairwell up to the roof of the building and told her everything I'd seen.
Look, it's a setback. I agree.
But the mask couldn't have concealed **everything**.
What color were his eyes?
Brown.
Probably.
I don't know. It was dark.
The whole thing was over so quickly.
Could you tell how old he was?
Well, he sprinted like an athlete, that's for sure.
I'm thinking he's still pretty young...
...but that's just a guess.
Maybe he doesn't always wear the mask.
Maybe next time you'll be able to see his face.

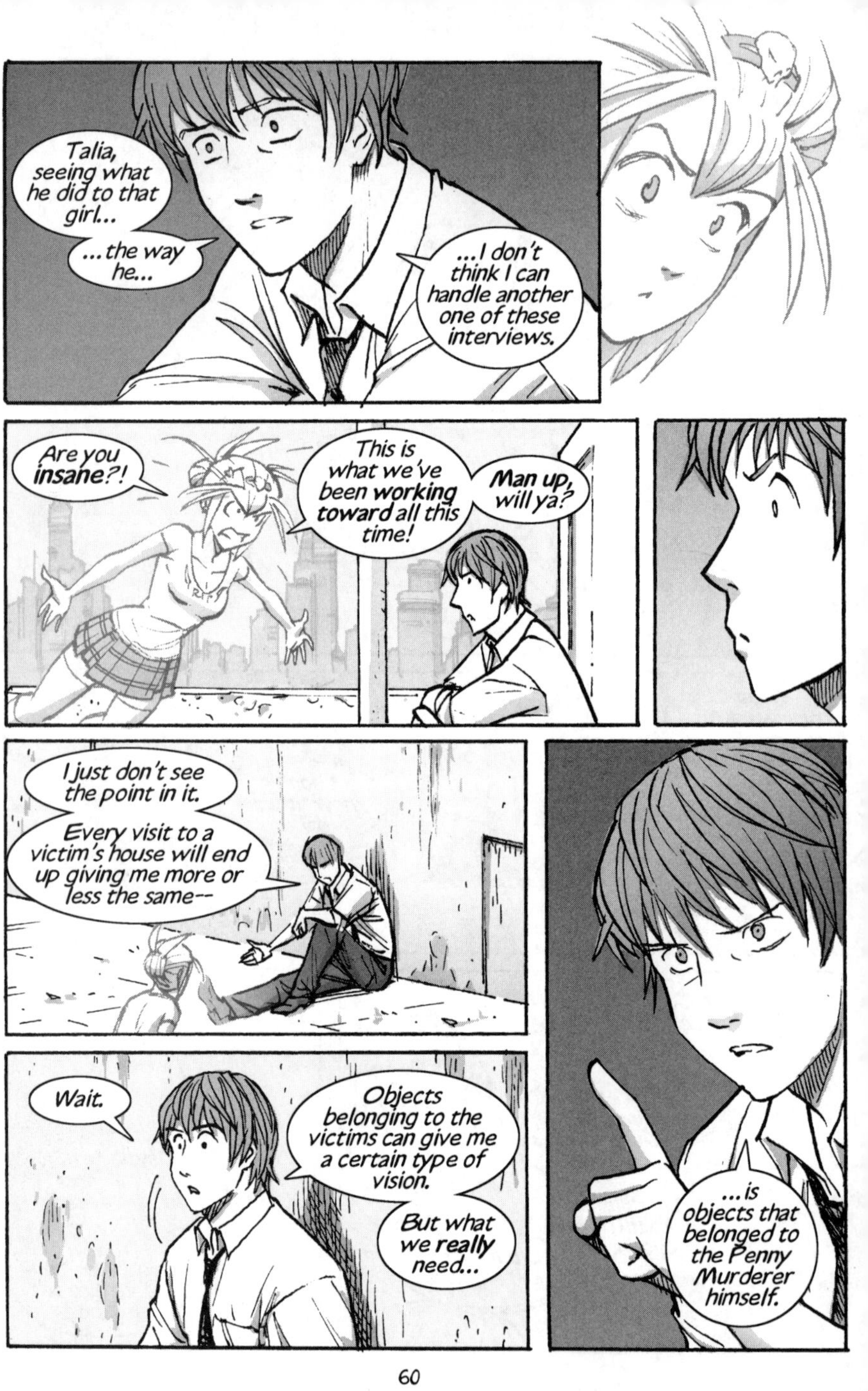

Talia, seeing what he did to that girl...
...the way he...
...I don't think I can handle another one of these interviews.
Are you **insane**?!
This is what we've been **working toward** all this time!
Man up, will ya?
I just don't see the point in it.
Every visit to a victim's house will end up giving me more or less the same--
Wait.
Objects belonging to the victims can give me a certain type of vision.
But what we **really** need...
...is objects that belonged to the Penny Murderer himself.

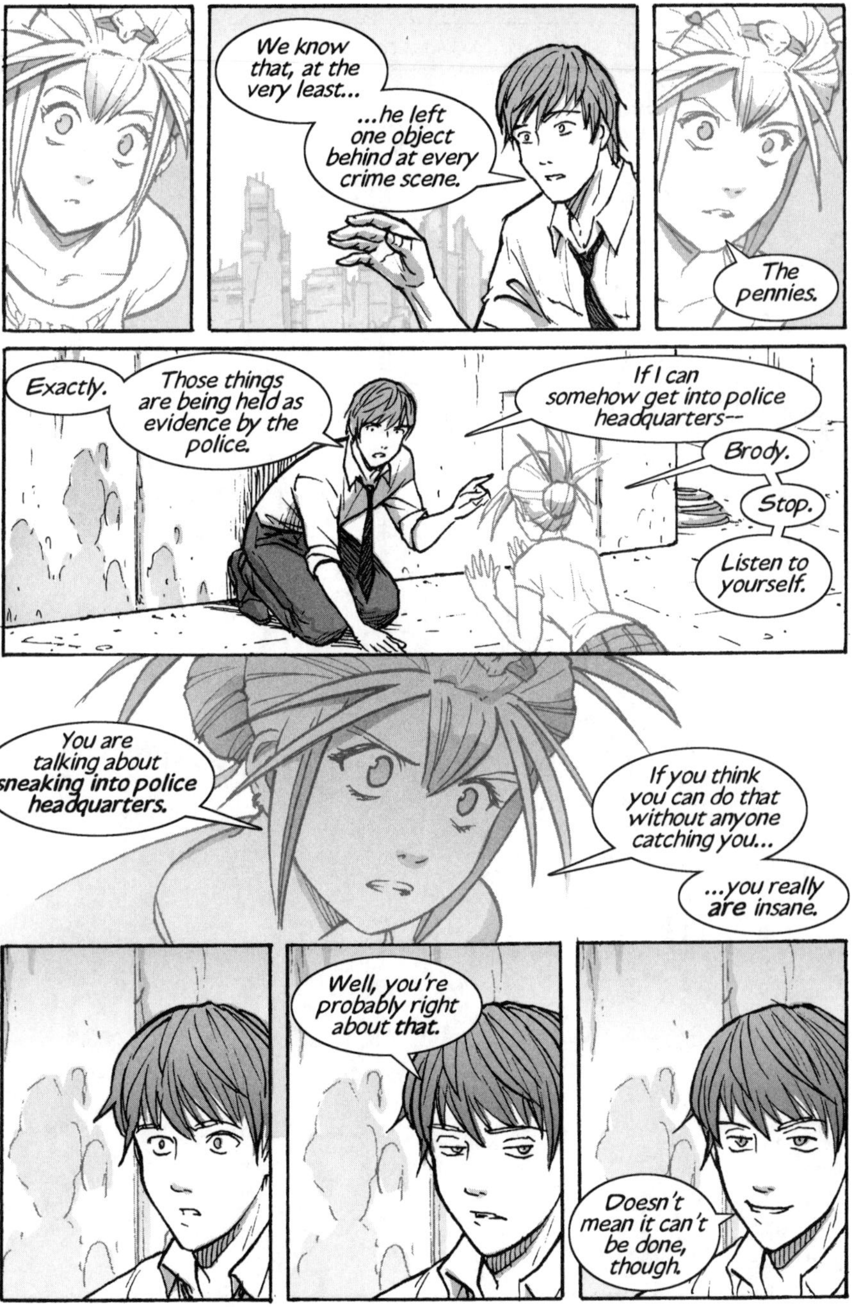
We know that, at the very least...
...he left one object behind at every crime scene.
The pennies.
Exactly.
Those things are being held as evidence by the police.
If I can somehow get into police headquarters--
Brody.
Stop.
Listen to yourself.
You are talking about sneaking into police headquarters.
If you think you can do that without anyone catching you...
...you really **are** insane.
Well, you're probably right about that.
Doesn't mean it can't be done, though.

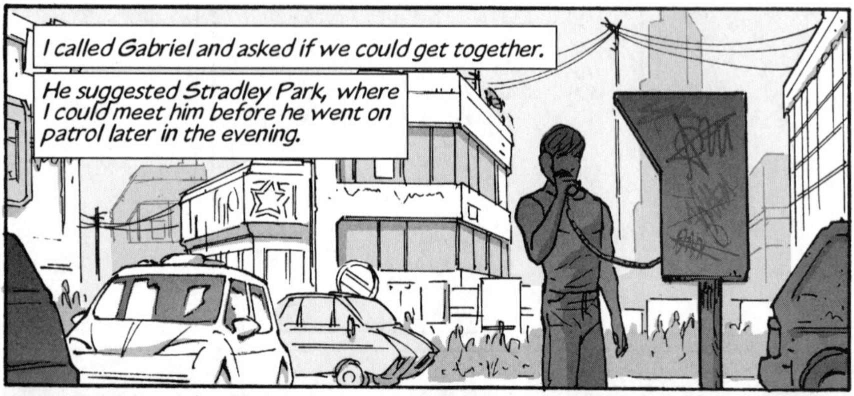
I called Gabriel and asked if we could get together.
He suggested Stradley Park, where I could meet him before he went on patrol later in the evening.

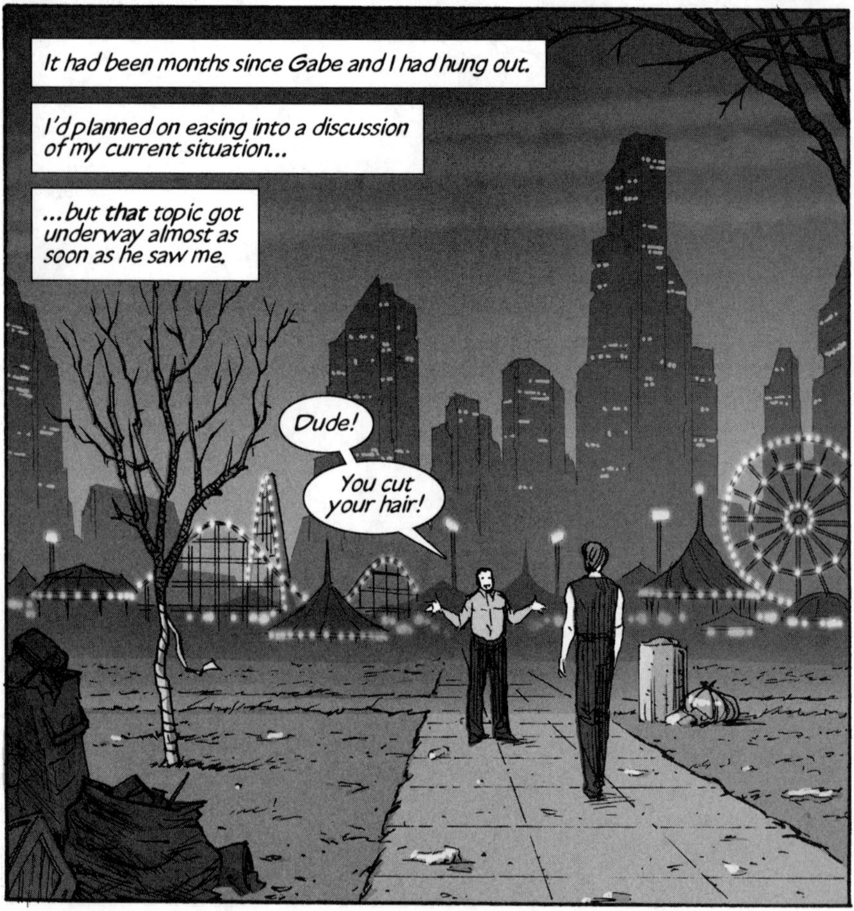
It had been months since Gabe and I had hung out.
I'd planned on easing into a discussion of my current situation...
...but that topic got underway almost as soon as he saw me.
Dude!
You cut your hair!

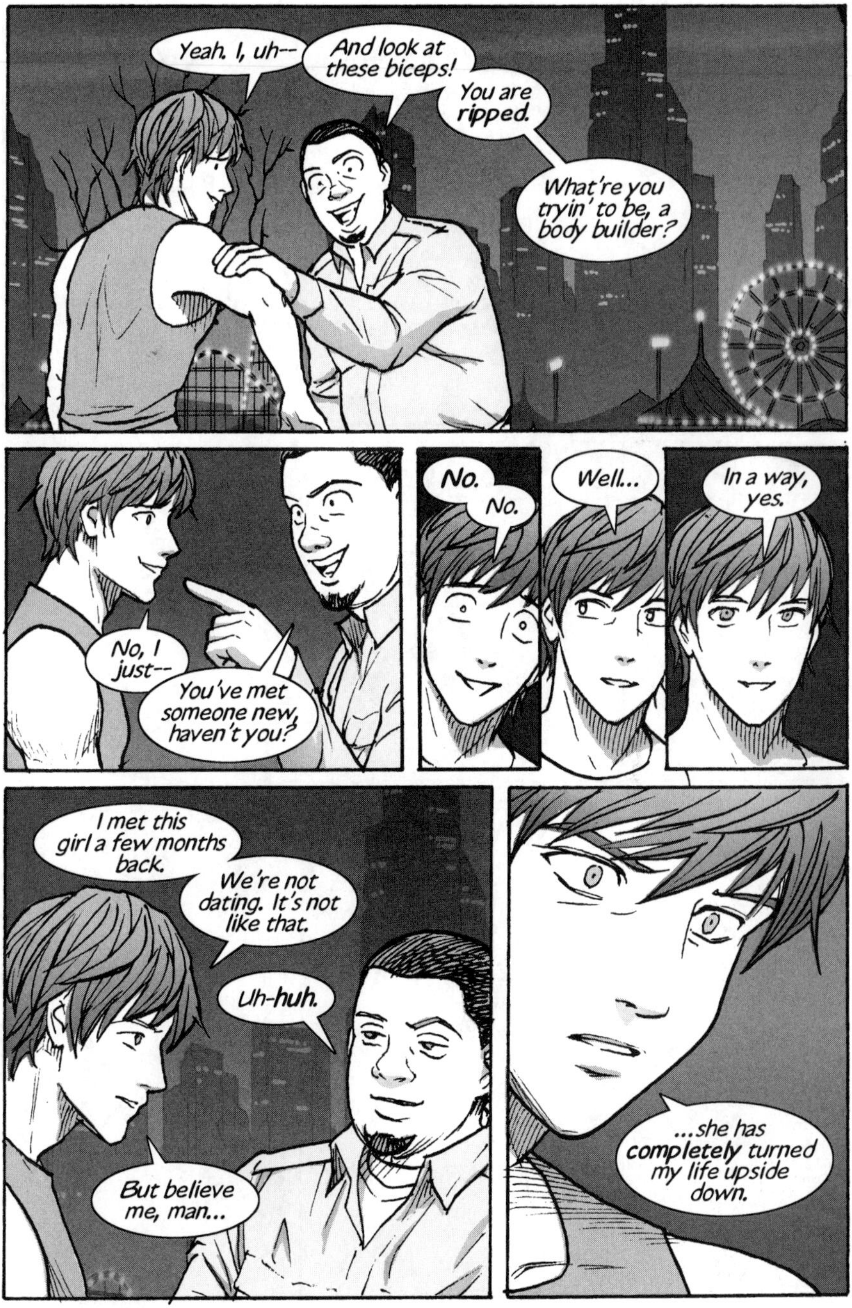
Yeah. I, uh--
And look at these biceps!
You are ripped.
What're you tryin' to be, a body builder?
No, I just--
You've met someone new, haven't you?
No.
No.
Well...
In a way, yes.
I met this girl a few months back.
We're not dating. It's not like that.
Uh-huh.
But believe me, man...
...she has completely turned my life upside down.

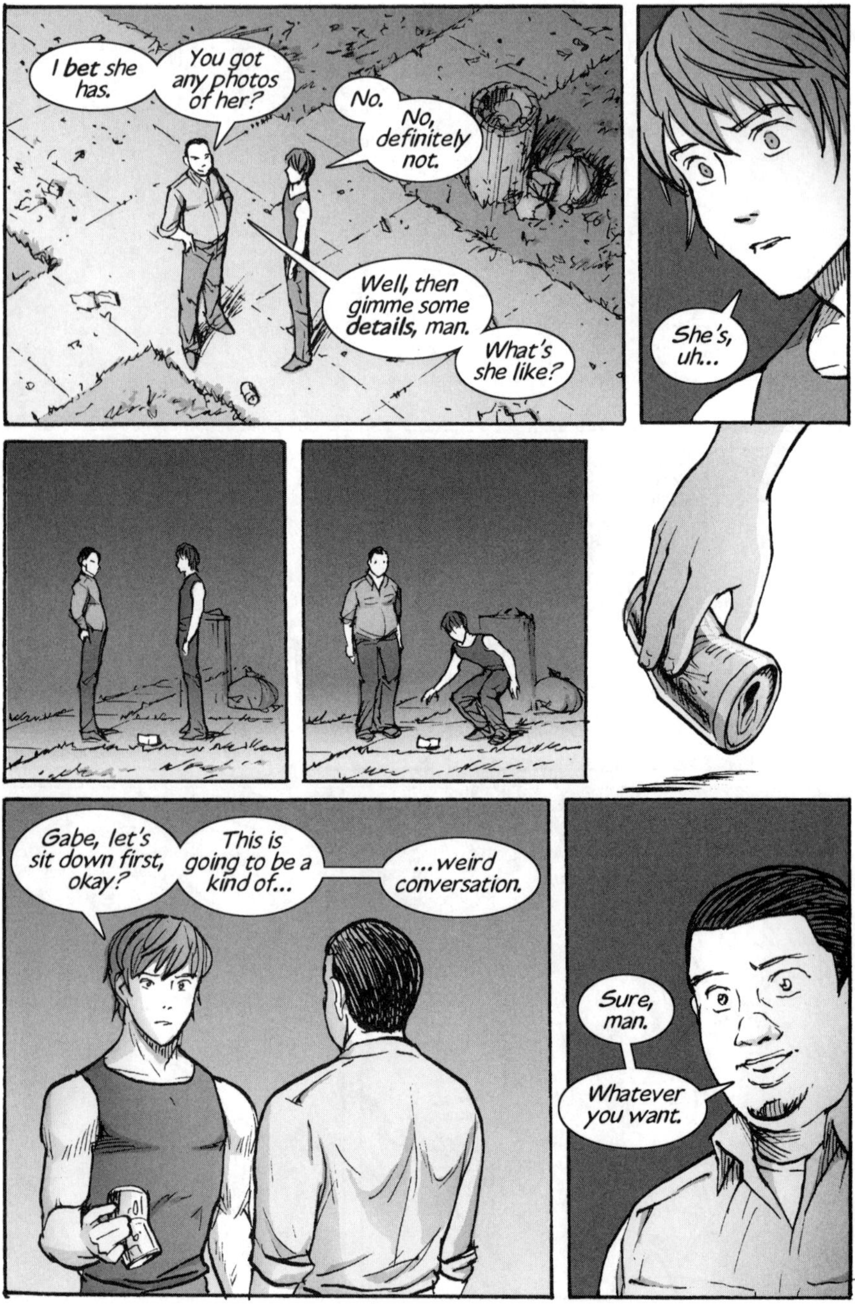
I bet she has.
You got any photos of her?
No.
No, definitely not.
Well, then gimme some details, man.
What's she like?
She's, uh...
Gabe, let's sit down first, okay?
This is going to be a kind of...
...weird conversation.
Sure, man.
Whatever you want.

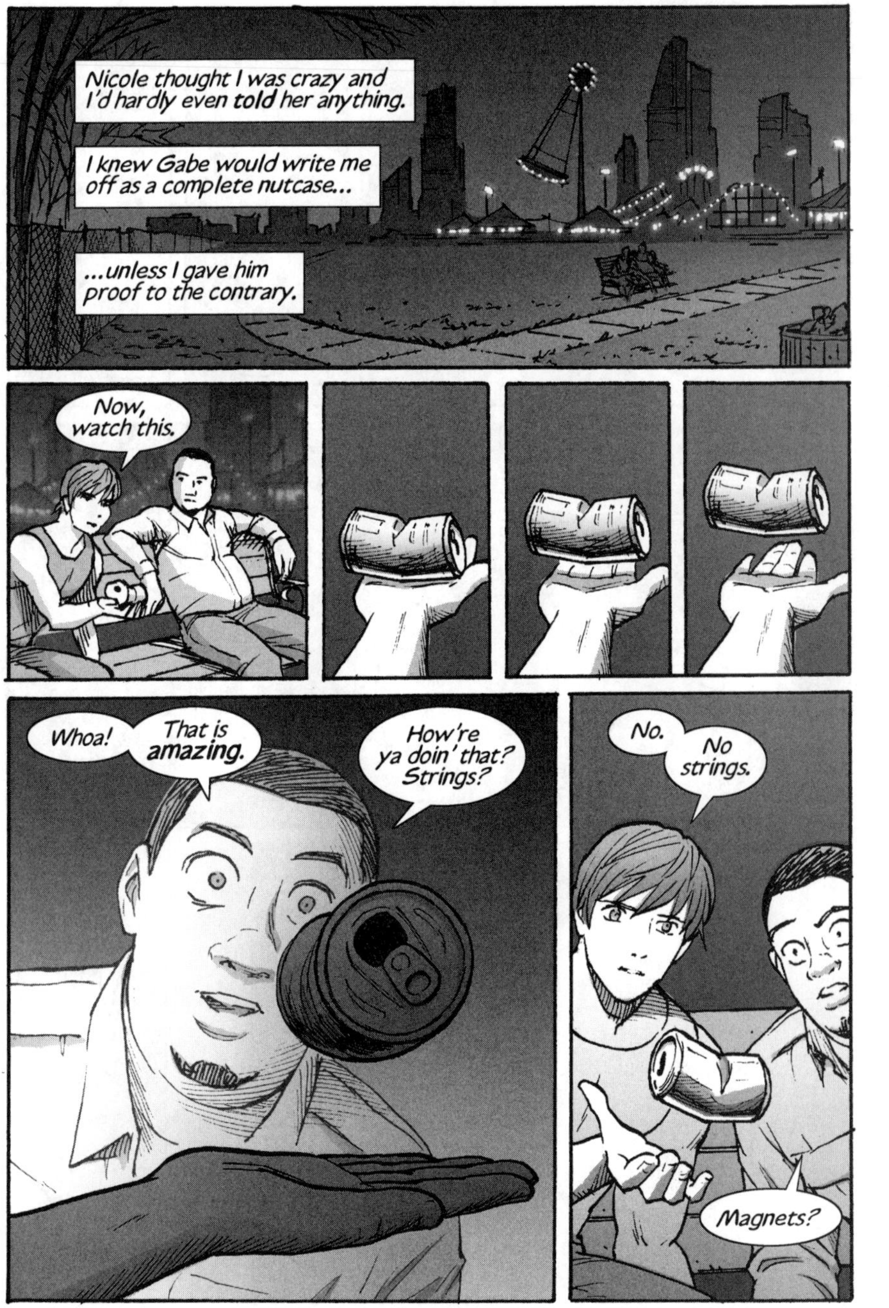
Nicole thought I was crazy and I'd hardly even **told** her anything.
I knew Gabe would write me off as a complete nutcase...
...unless I gave him proof to the contrary.
Now, watch this.
Whoa!
That is **amazing.**
How're ya doin' that? Strings?
No.
No strings.
Magnets?

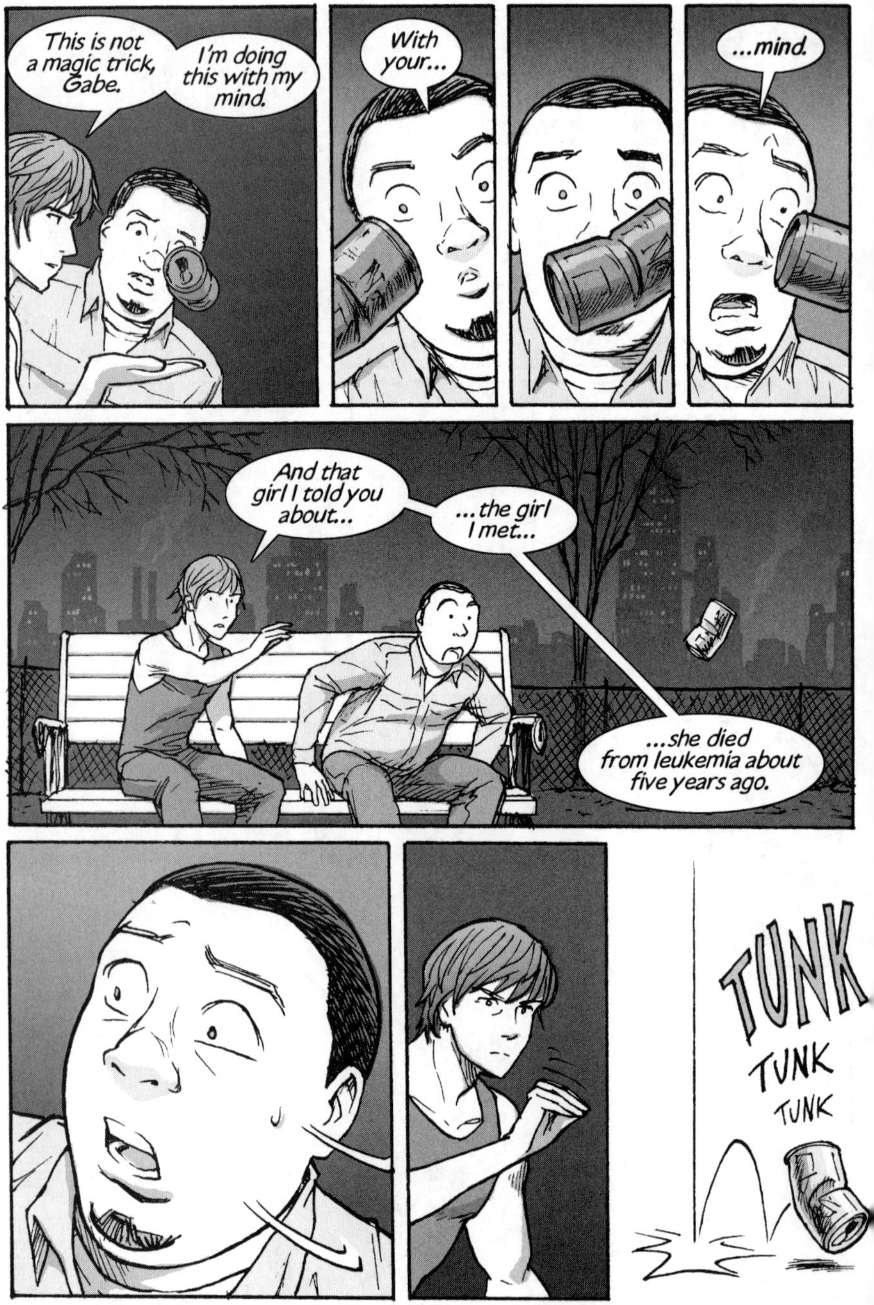
This is not a magic trick, Gabe.
I'm doing this with my mind.
With your...
...mind.
And that girl I told you about...
...the girl I met...
...she died from leukemia about five years ago.
TUNK
TUNK
TUNK

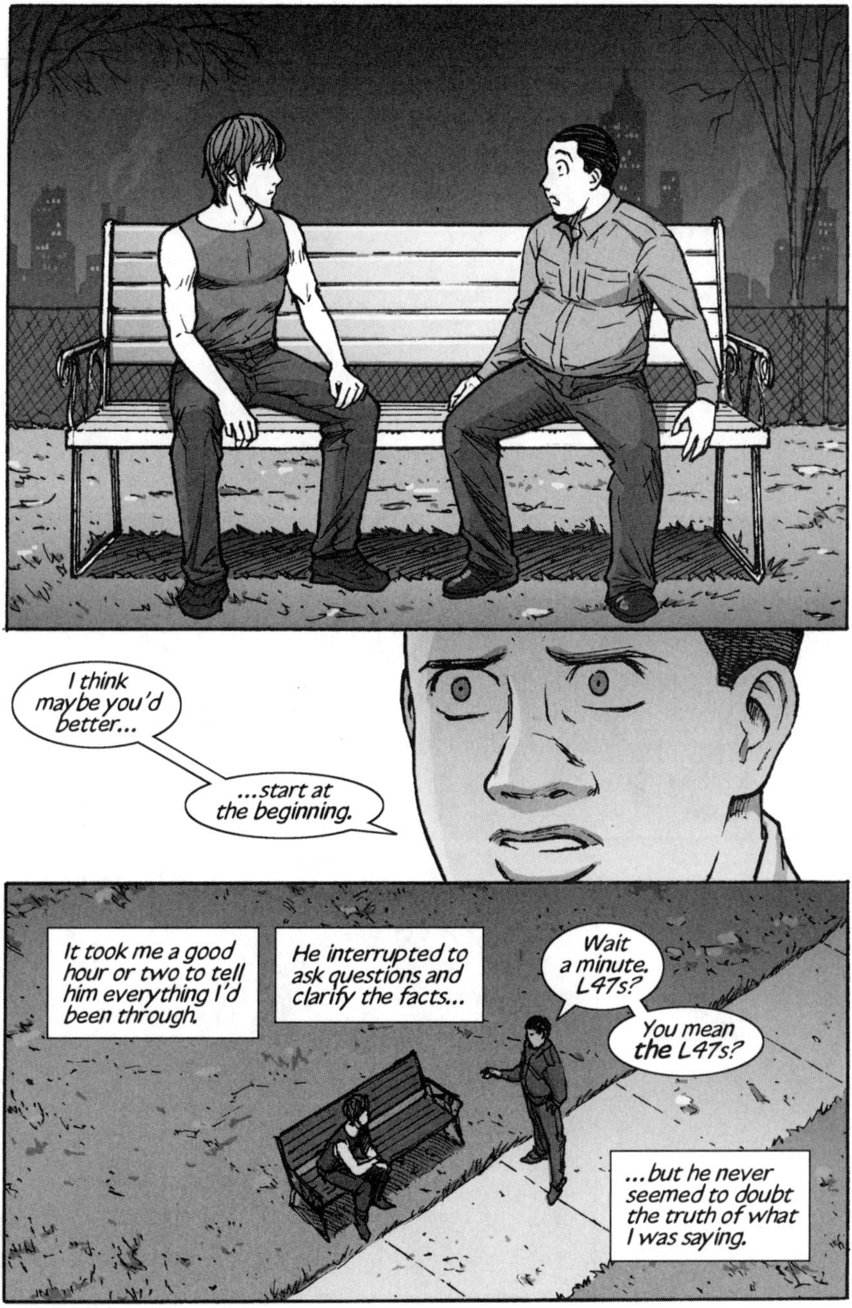
I think maybe you'd better...
...start at the beginning.
It took me a good hour or two to tell him everything I'd been through.
He interrupted to ask questions and clarify the facts...
Wait a minute. L47s?
You mean the L47s?
...but he never seemed to doubt the truth of what I was saying.

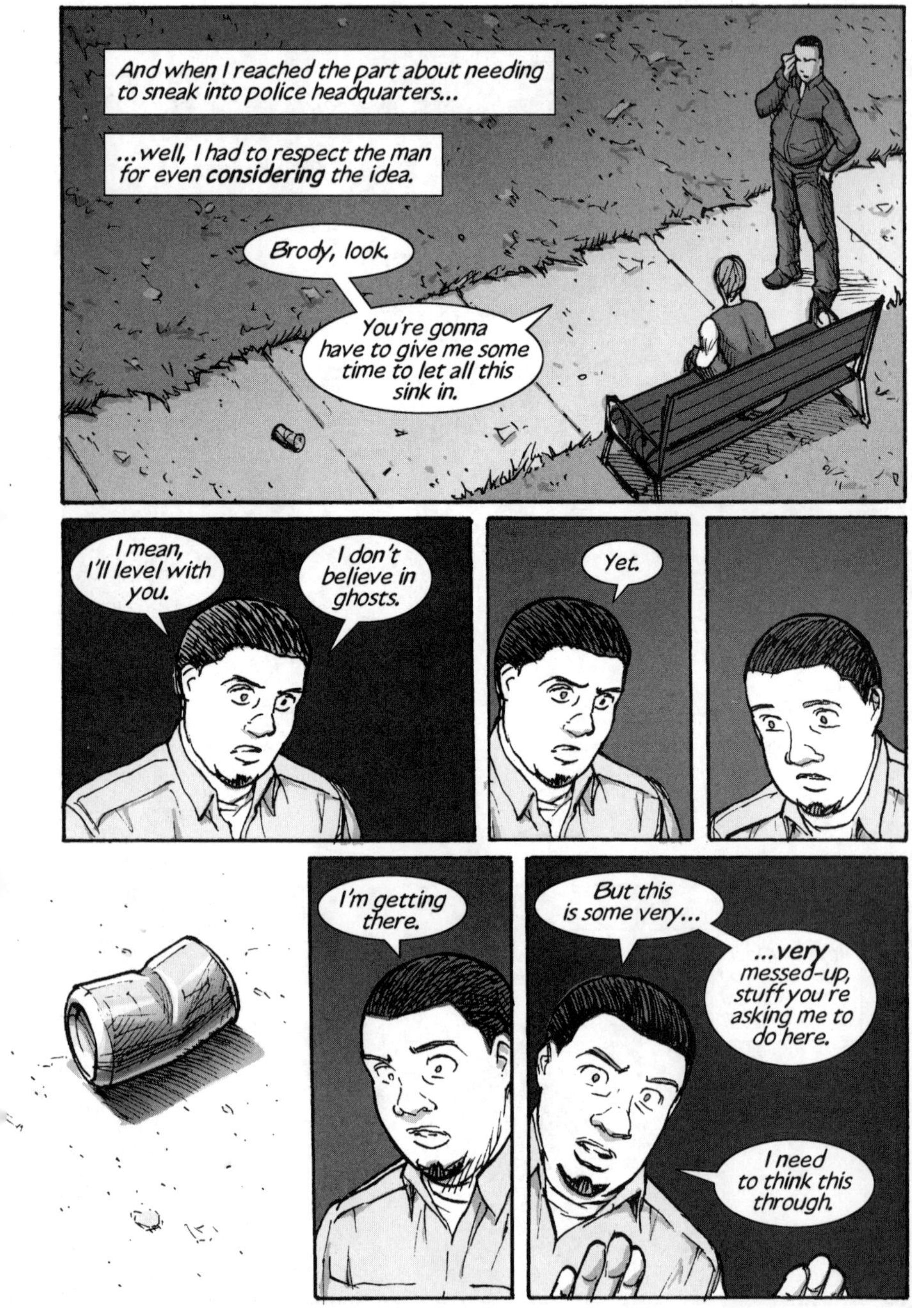

And when I reached the part about needing to sneak into police headquarters...
...well, I had to respect the man for even **considering** the idea.
Brody, look.
You're gonna have to give me some time to let all this sink in.
I mean, I'll level with you.
I don't believe in ghosts.
Yet.
I'm getting there.
But this is some very...
...**very** messed-up, stuff you're asking me to do here.
I need to think this through.

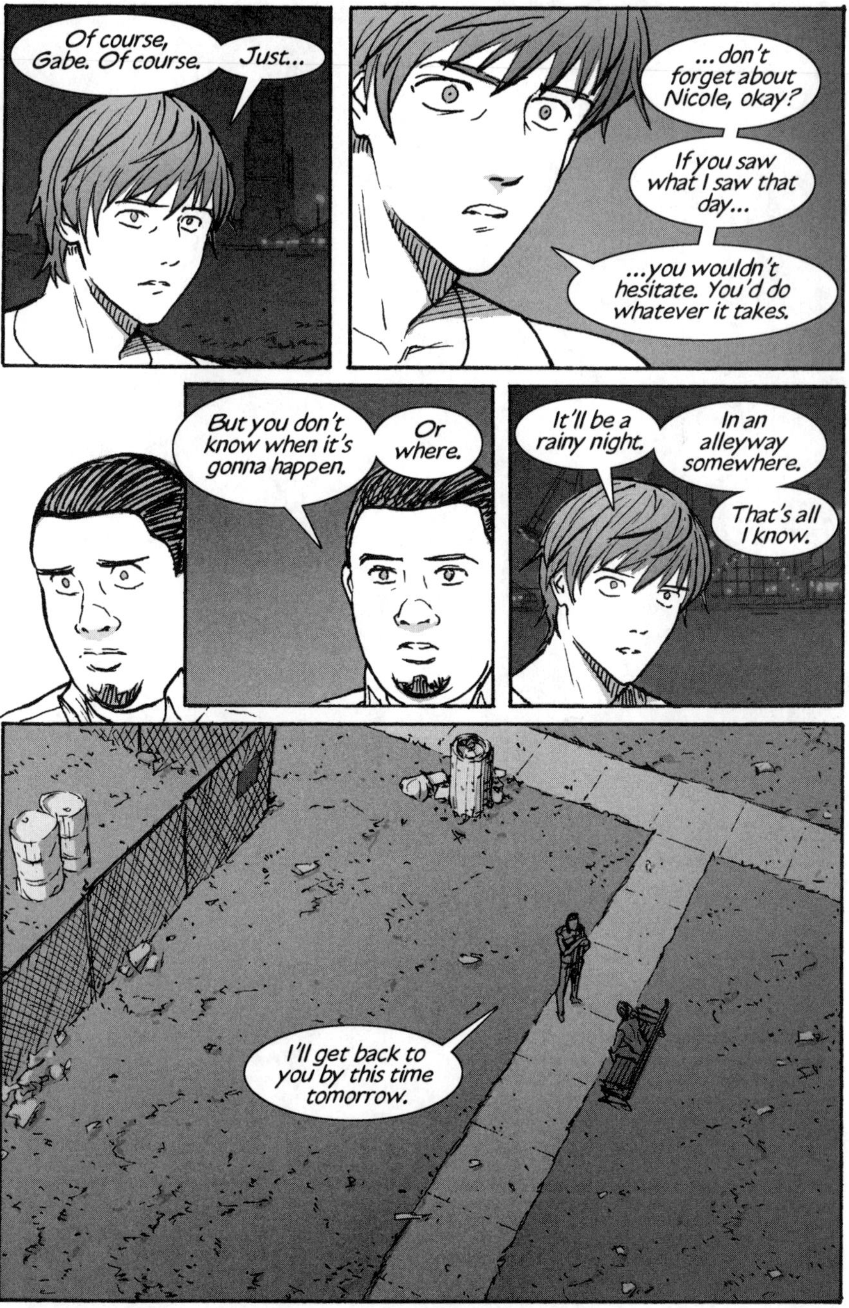
Of course, Gabe. Of course.
Just...
...don't forget about Nicole, okay?
If you saw what I saw that day...
...you wouldn't hesitate. You'd do whatever it takes.
But you don't know when it's gonna happen.
Or where.
It'll be a rainy night.
In an alleyway somewhere.
That's all I know.
I'll get back to you by this time tomorrow.

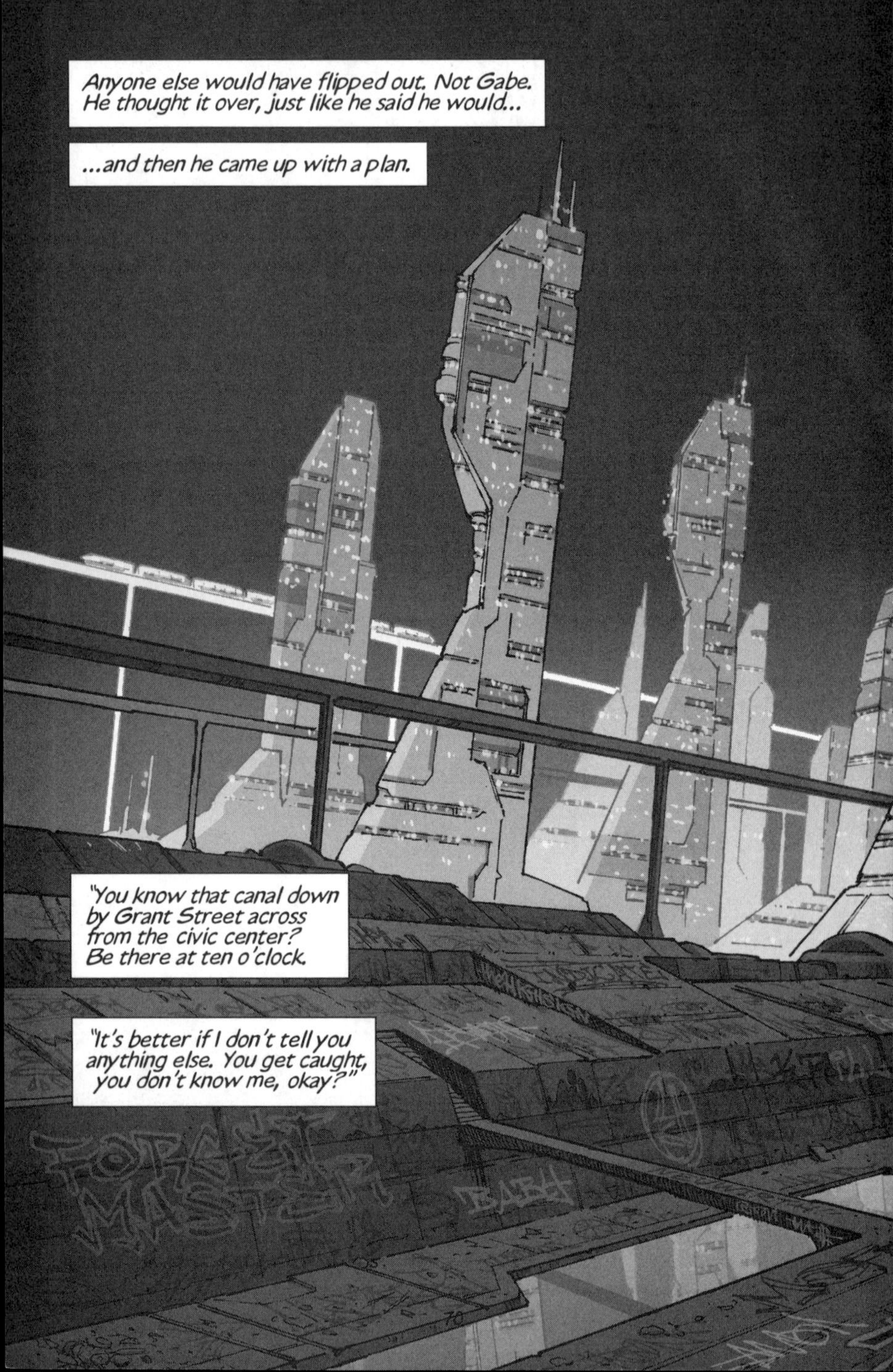
Anyone else would have flipped out. Not Gabe. He thought it over, just like he said he would...
...and then he came up with a plan.
"You know that canal down by Grant Street across from the civic center? Be there at ten o'clock.
"It's better if I don't tell you anything else. You get caught, you don't know me, okay?"

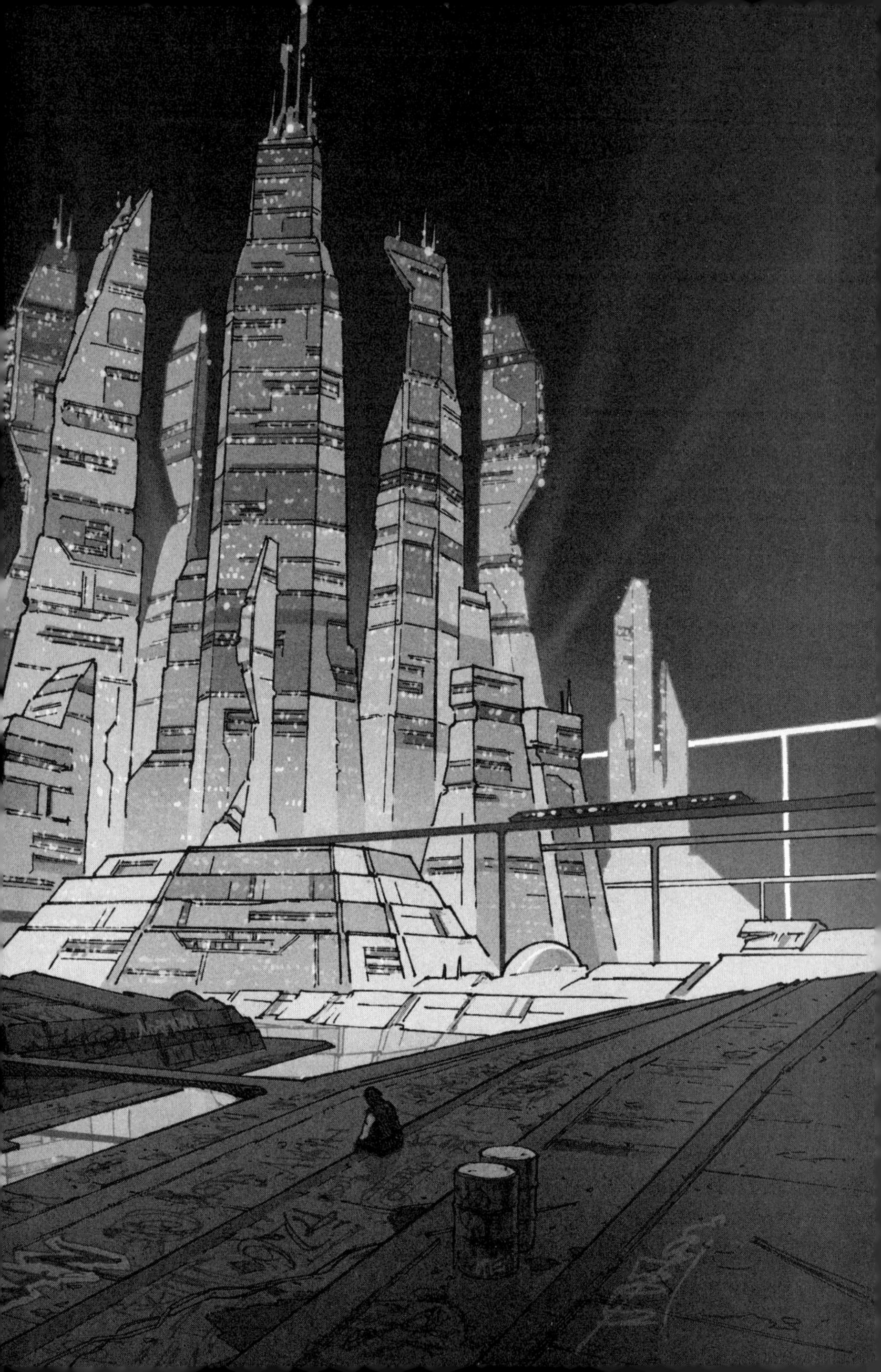

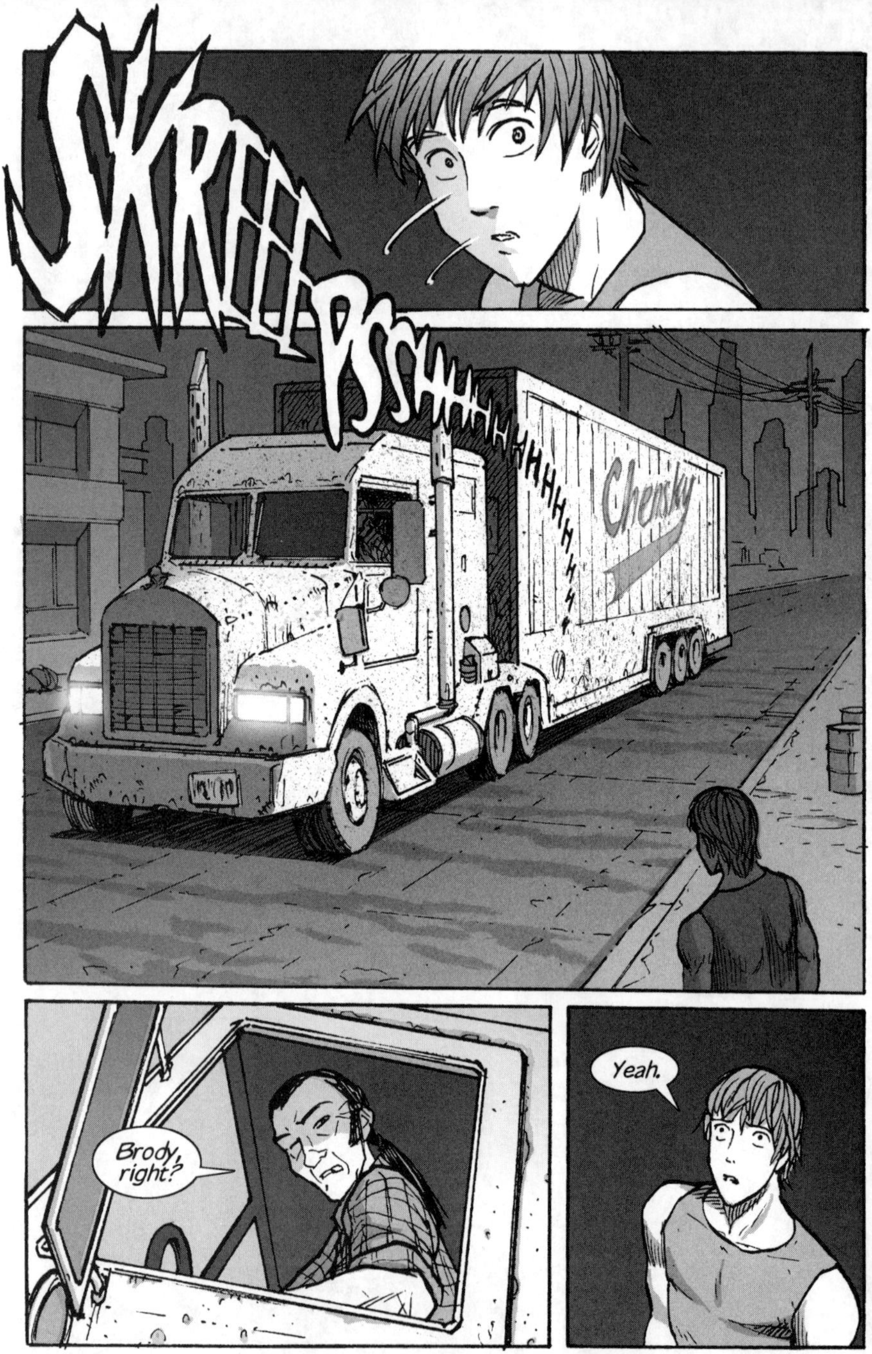
SKREEE
PSSHHHHHHHHHHHHHHHHH
Chensky
Brody, right?
Yeah.

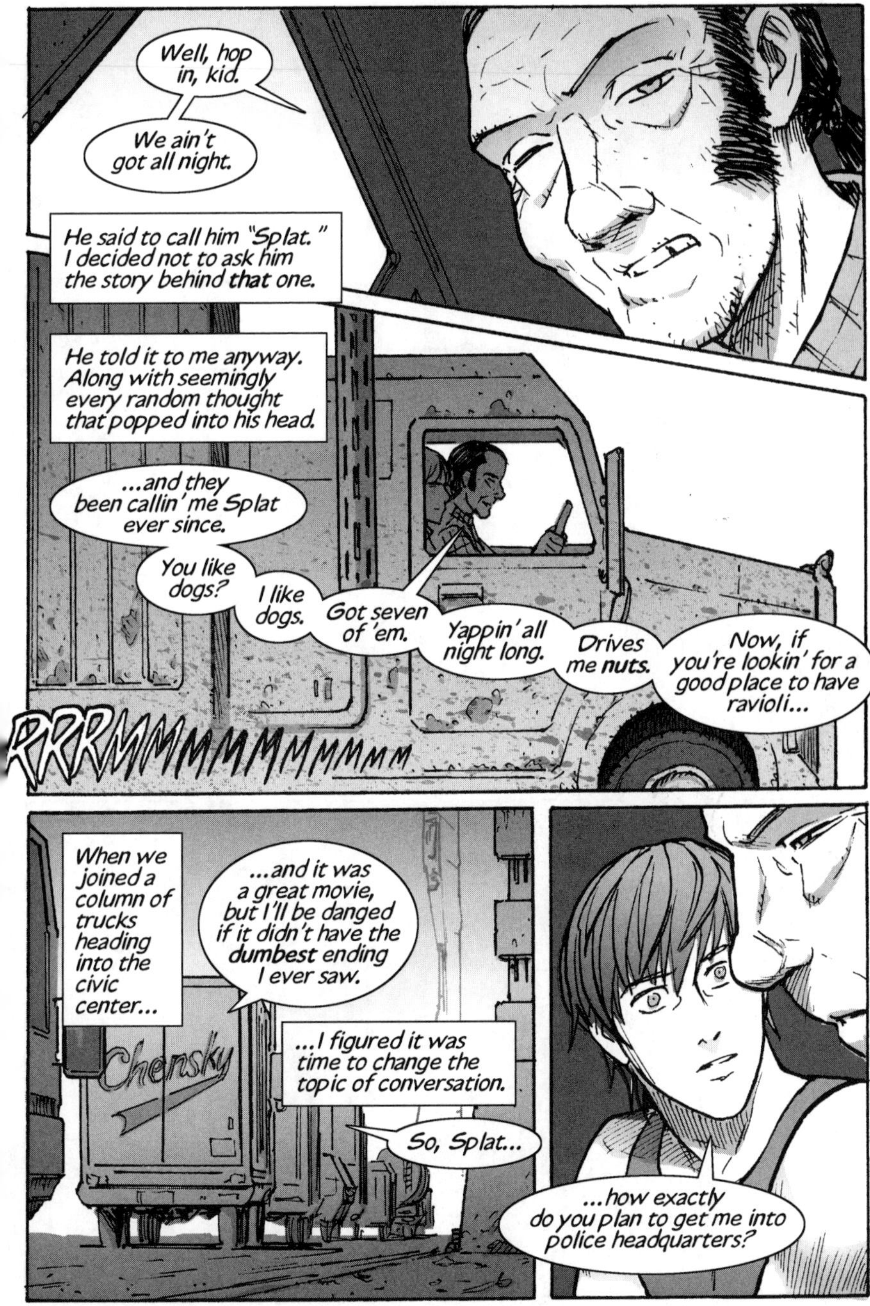

Well, hop in, kid.
We ain't got all night.
He said to call him "Splat." I decided not to ask him the story behind **that** one.
He told it to me anyway. Along with seemingly every random thought that popped into his head.
...and they been callin' me Splat ever since.
You like dogs?
I like dogs.
Got seven of 'em.
Yappin' all night long.
Drives me **nuts**.
Now, if you're lookin' for a good place to have ravioli...
RRRMMMMMMMMMMMM
When we joined a column of trucks heading into the civic center...
...and it was a great movie, but I'll be danged if it didn't have the **dumbest** ending I ever saw.
Chensky
...I figured it was time to change the topic of conversation.
So, Splat...
...how exactly do you plan to get me into police headquarters?

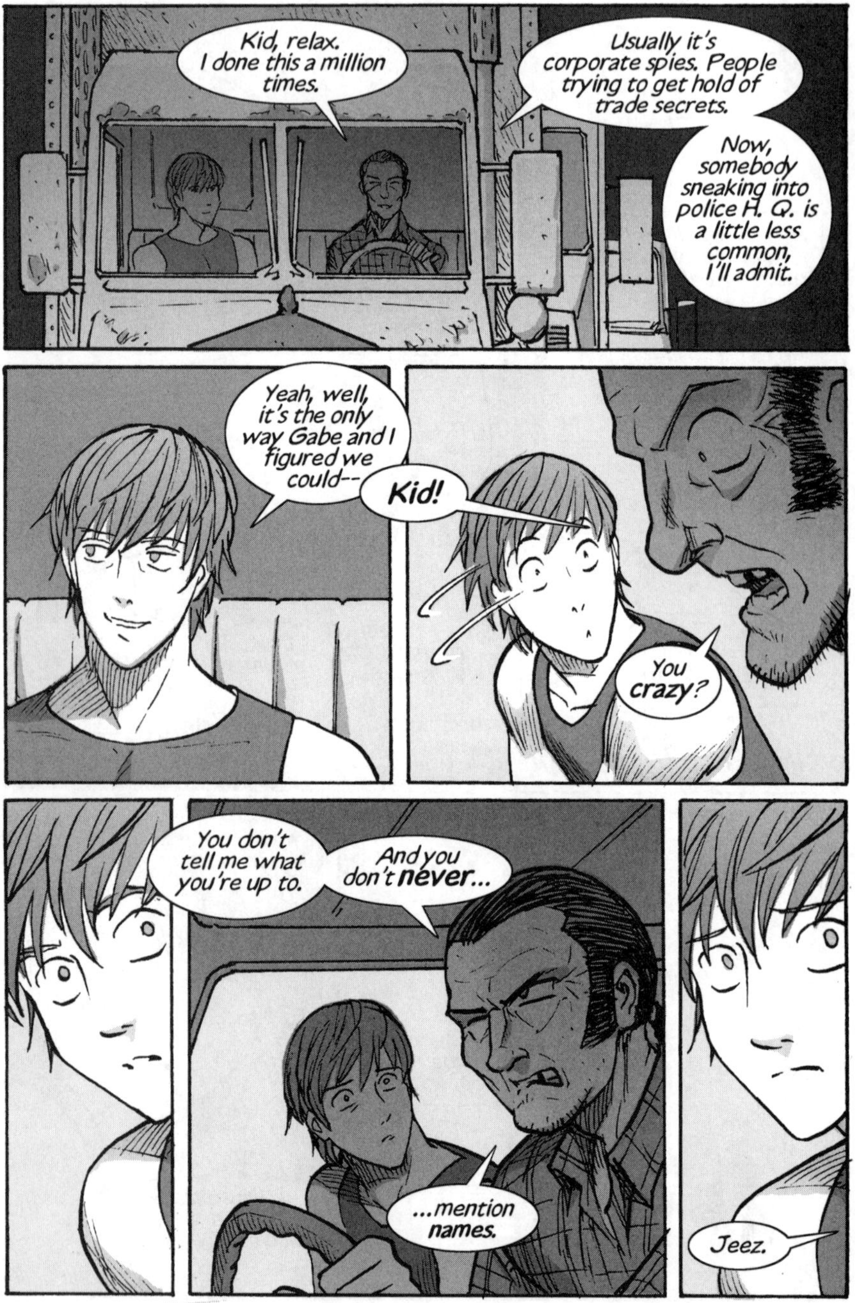
Kid, relax. I done this a million times.
Usually it's corporate spies. People trying to get hold of trade secrets.
Now, somebody sneaking into police H. Q. is a little less common, I'll admit.
Yeah, well, it's the only way Gabe and I figured we could--
Kid!
You **crazy**?
You don't tell me what you're up to.
And you don't **never**...
...mention **names**.
Jeez.

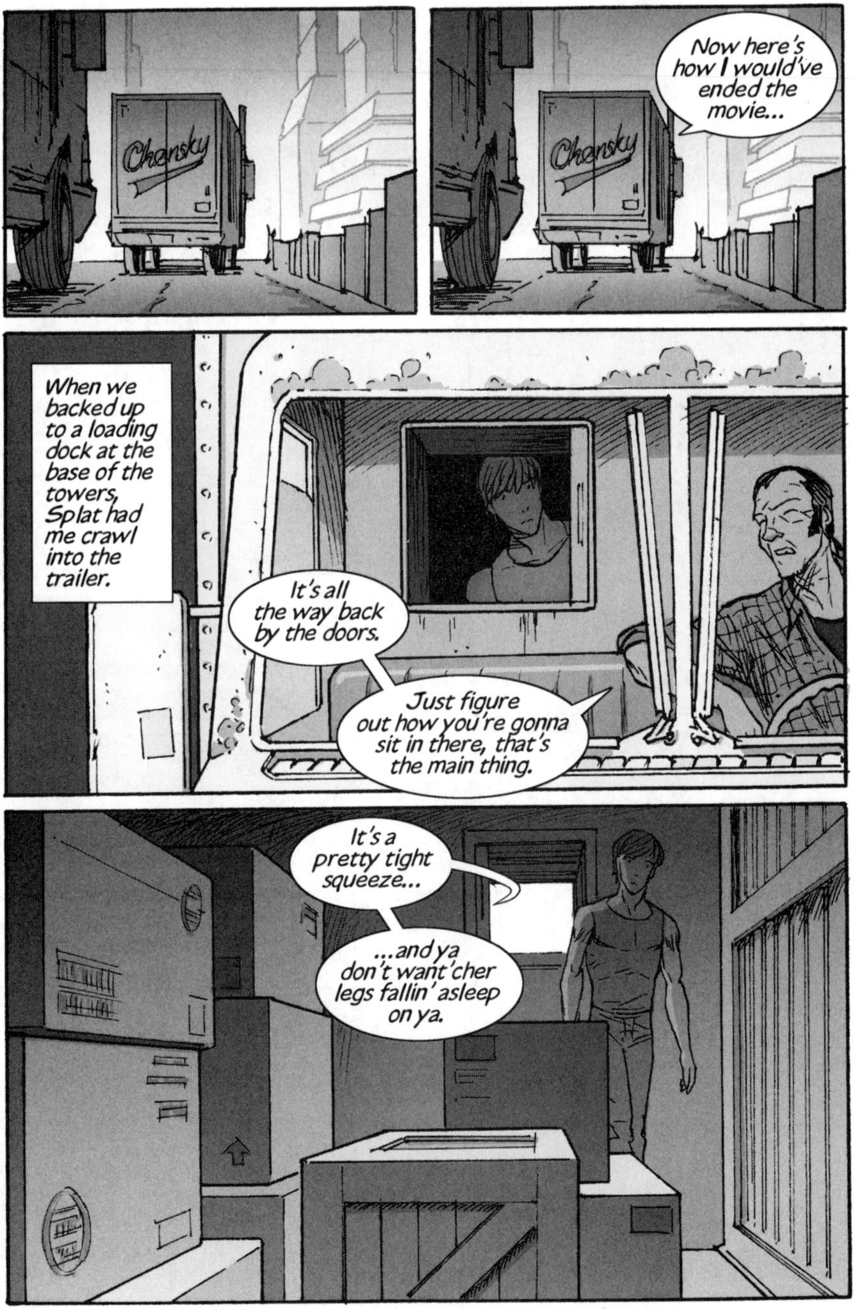
Chonsky
Chonsky
Now here's how I would've ended the movie...
When we backed up to a loading dock at the base of the towers, Splat had me crawl into the trailer.
It's all the way back by the doors.
Just figure out how you're gonna sit in there, that's the main thing.
It's a pretty tight squeeze...
...and ya don't want'cher legs fallin' asleep on ya.

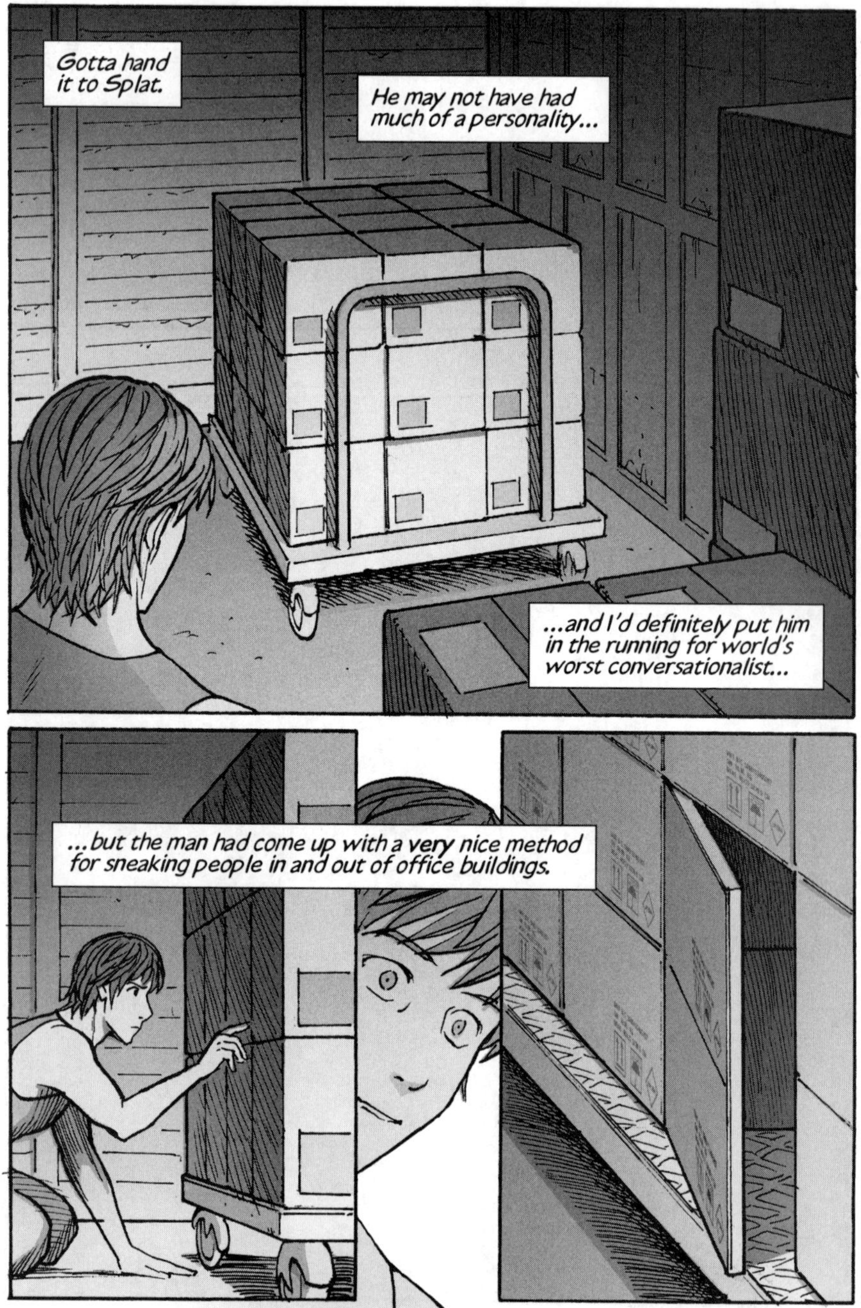
Gotta hand it to Splat.
He may not have had much of a personality...
...and I'd definitely put him in the running for world's worst conversationalist...
...but the man had come up with a very nice method for sneaking people in and out of office buildings.

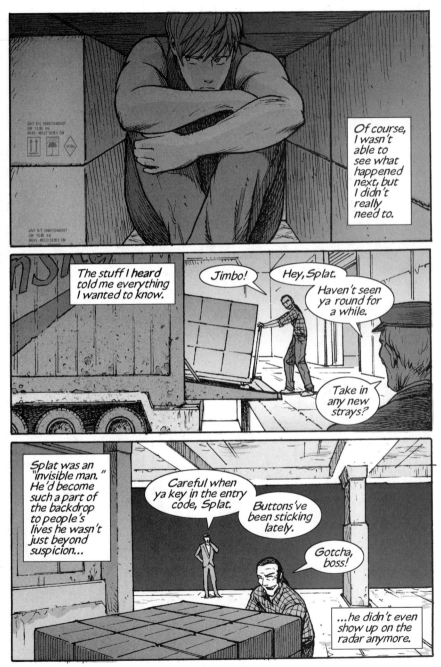

Of course, I wasn't able to see what happened next, but I didn't really need to.

The stuff I *heard* told me everything I wanted to know.

Jimbo!

Hey, Splat. Haven't seen ya round for a while.

Take in any new strays?

Splat was an "invisible man." He'd become such a part of the backdrop to people's lives he wasn't just beyond suspicion...

Careful when ya key in the entry code, Splat.

Buttons've been sticking lately.

Gotcha, boss!

...he didn't even show up on the radar anymore.

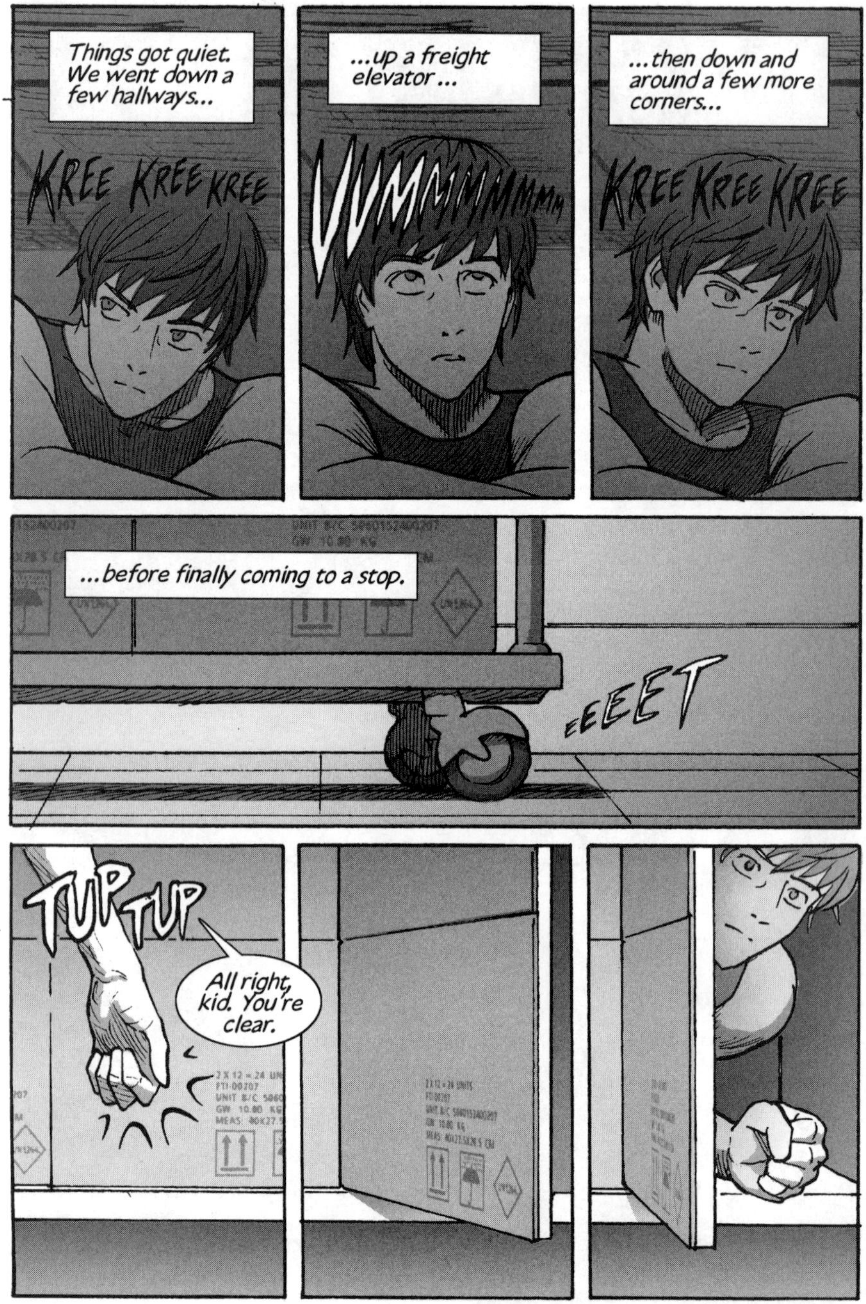
Things got quiet. We went down a few hallways...
KREE KREE KREE
...up a freight elevator...
VVMMMMMMMM
...then down and around a few more corners...
KREE KREE KREE
...before finally coming to a stop.
EEEET
TUP TUP
All right, kid. You're clear.

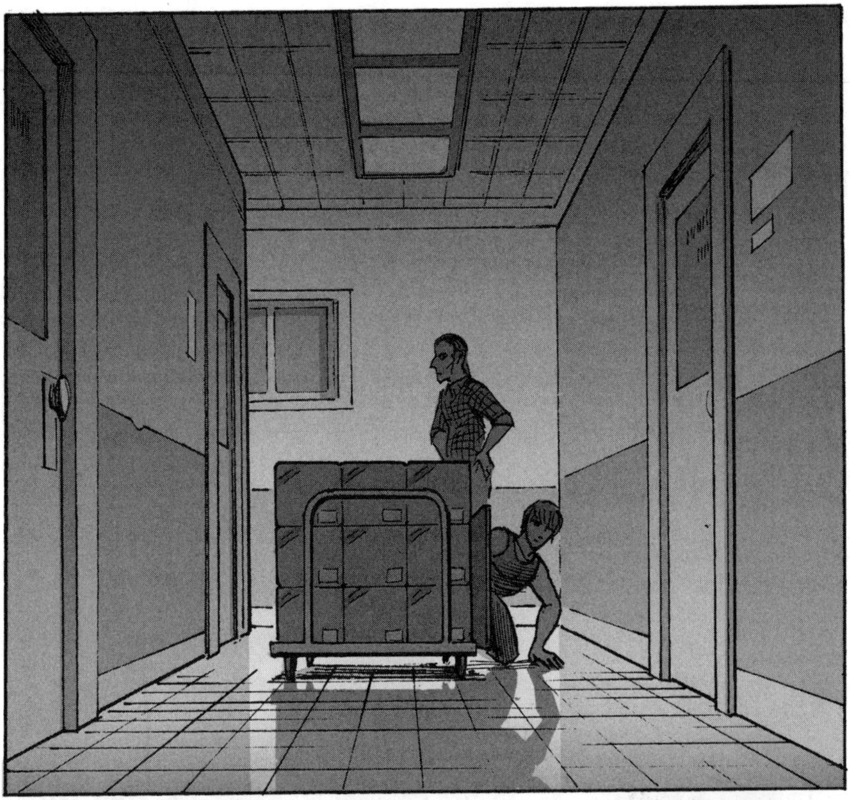

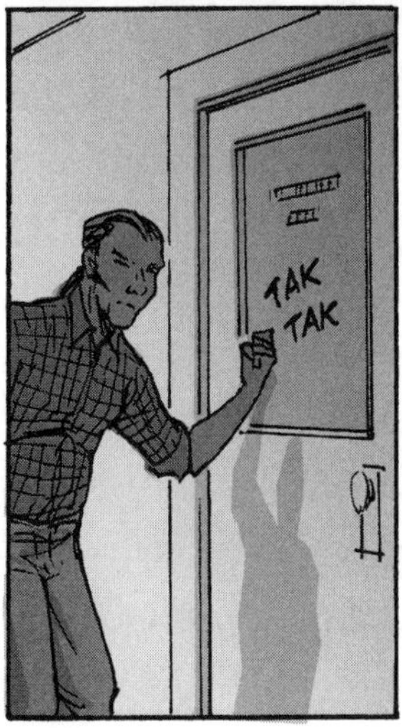
TAK
TAK

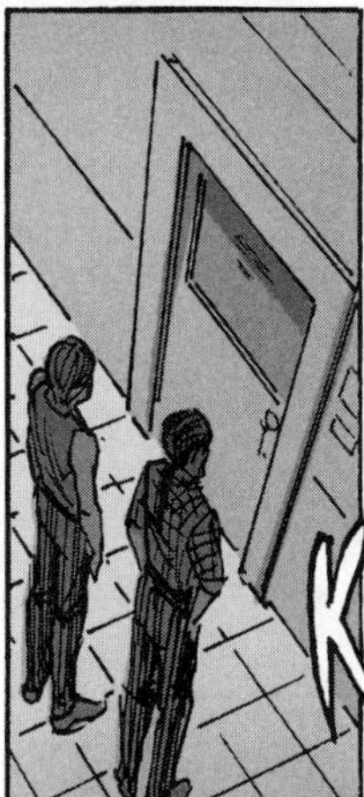

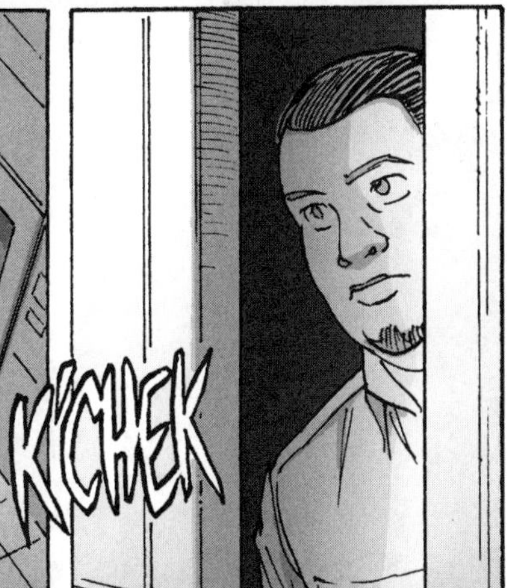
K'CHEK

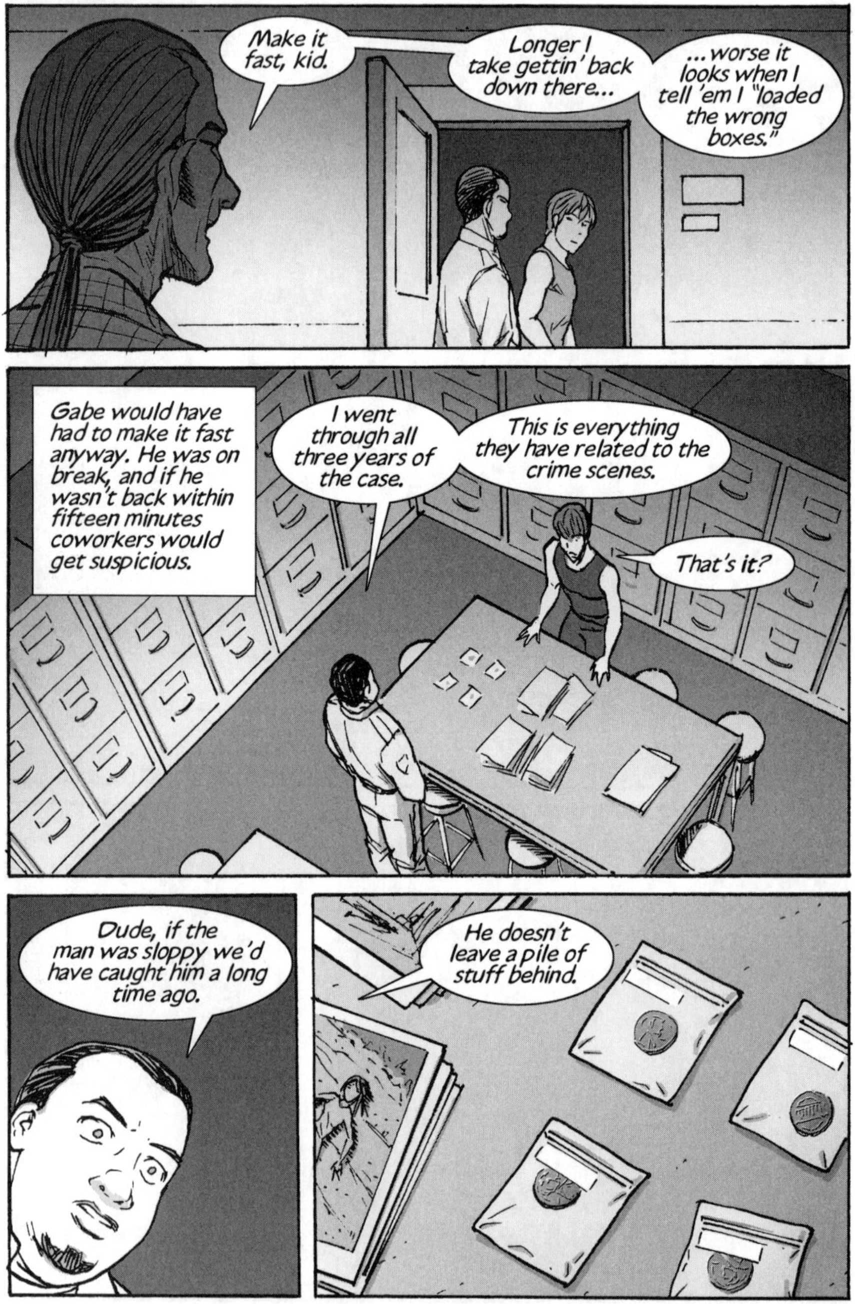
Make it fast, kid.
Longer I take gettin' back down there...
...worse it looks when I tell 'em I "loaded the wrong boxes."
Gabe would have had to make it fast anyway. He was on break, and if he wasn't back within fifteen minutes coworkers would get suspicious.
I went through all three years of the case.
This is everything they have related to the crime scenes.
That's it?
Dude, if the man was sloppy we'd have caught him a long time ago.
He doesn't leave a pile of stuff behind.

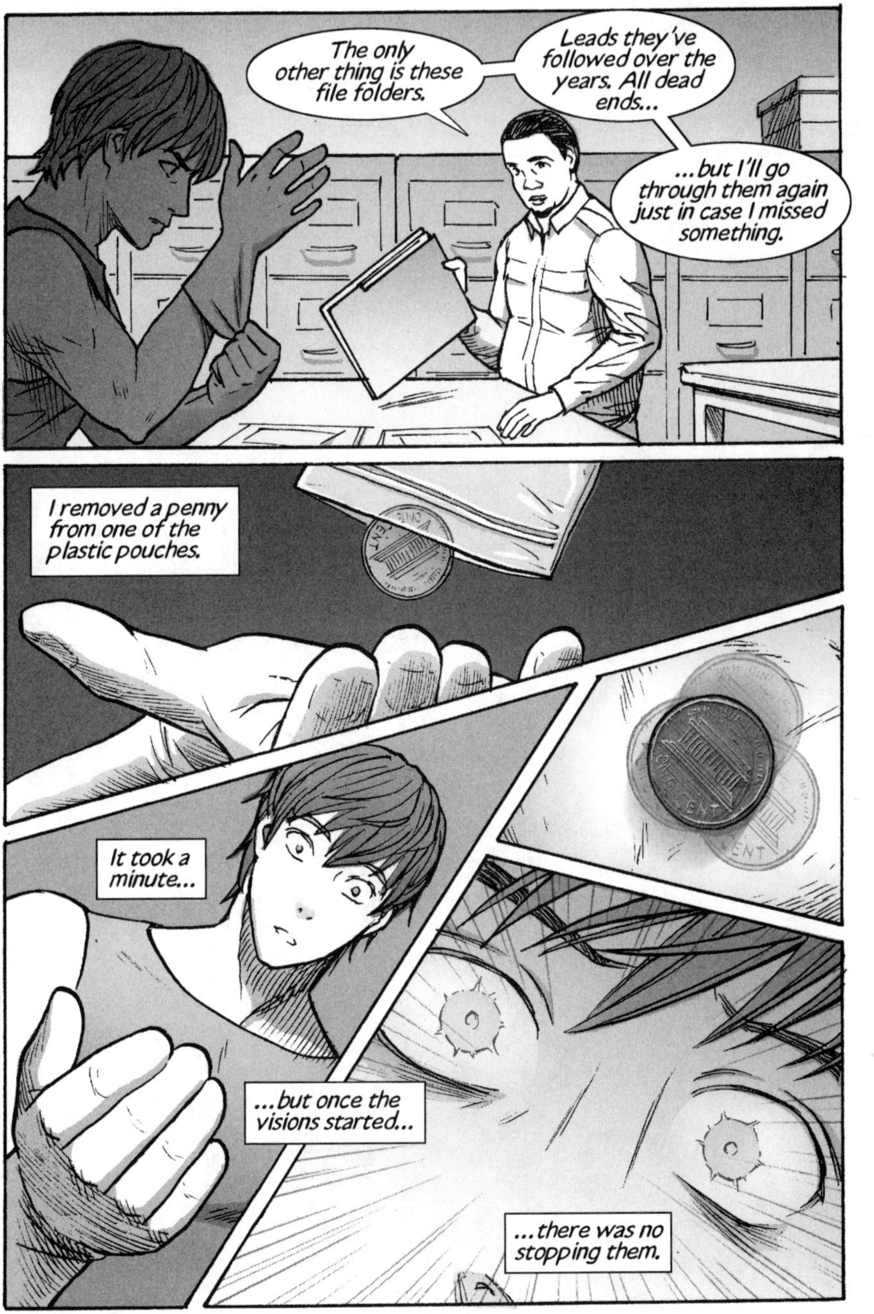
The only other thing is these file folders.
Leads they've followed over the years. All dead ends...
...but I'll go through them again just in case I missed something.
I removed a penny from one of the plastic pouches.
It took a minute...
...but once the visions started...
...there was no stopping them.

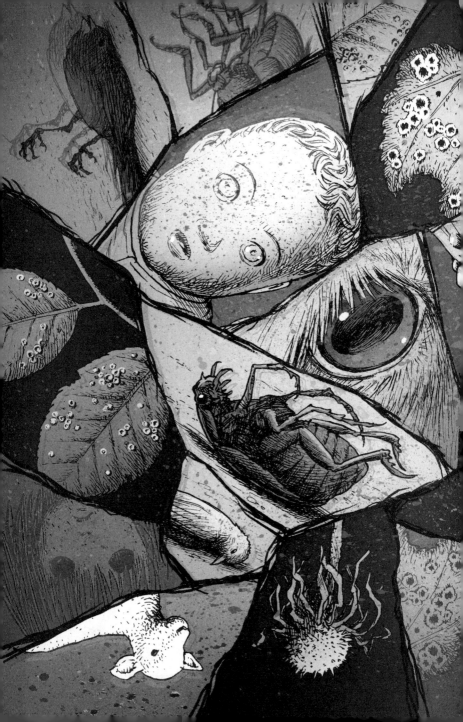

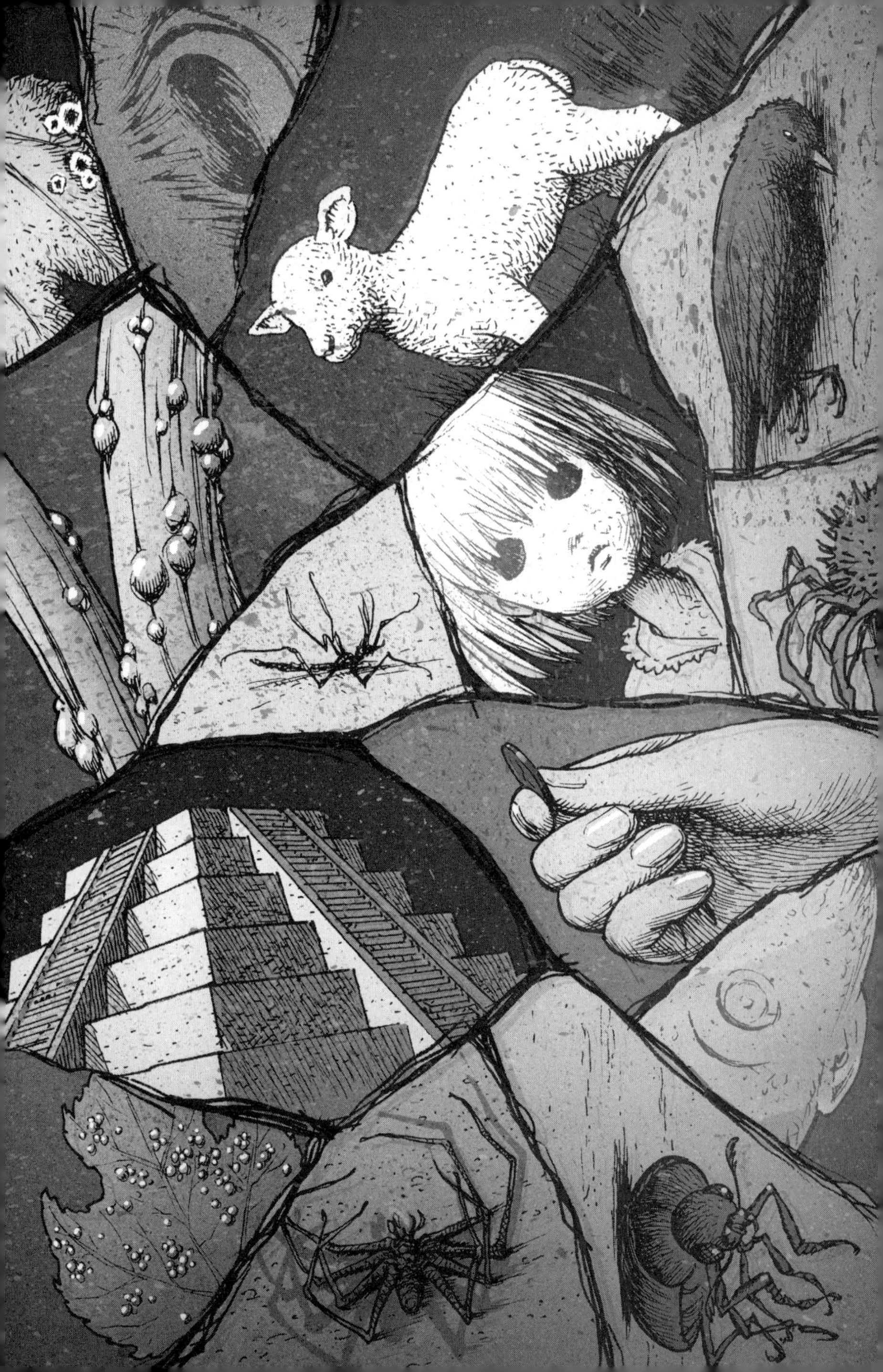

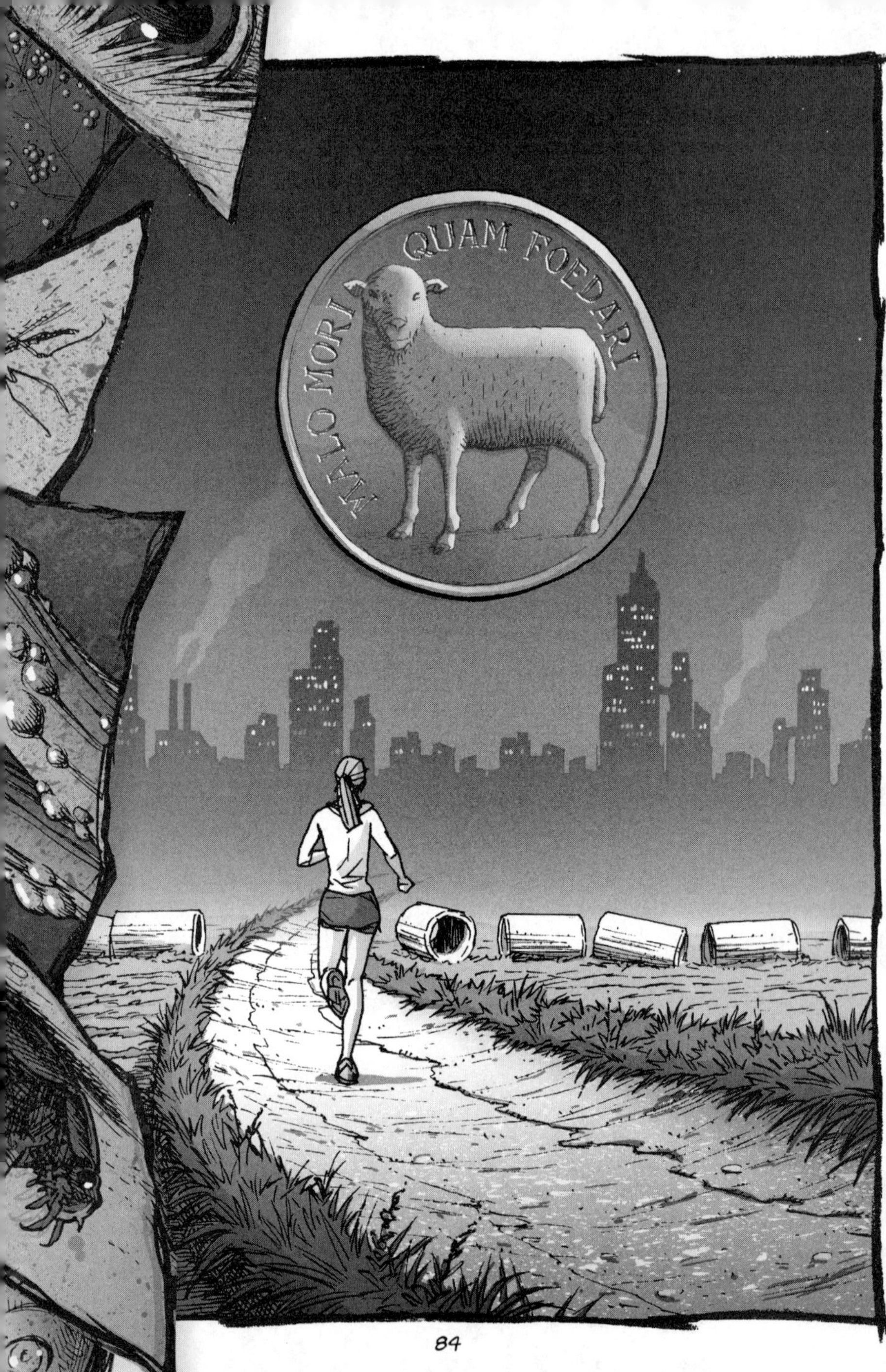
MALO MORI QUAM FOEDARI

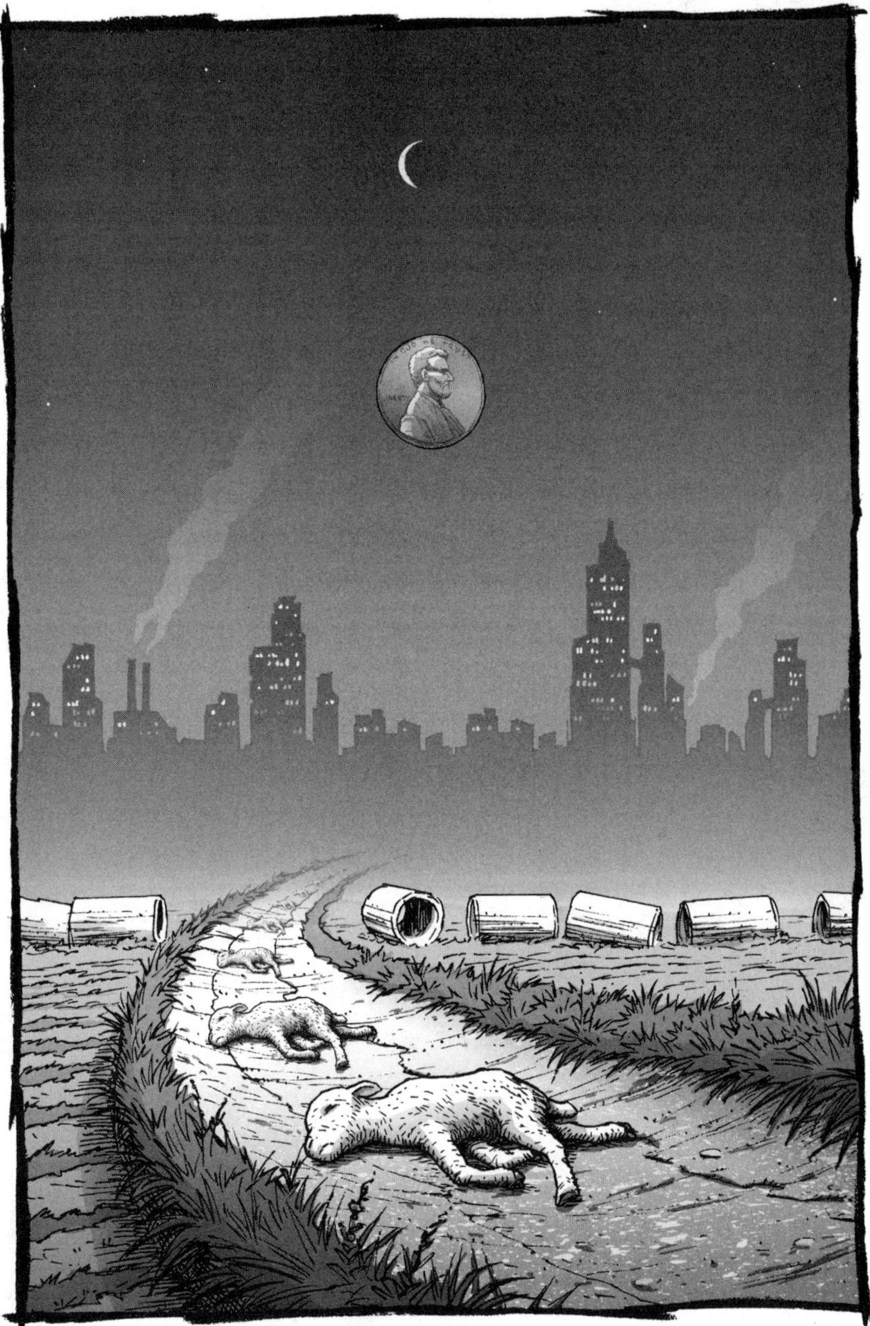

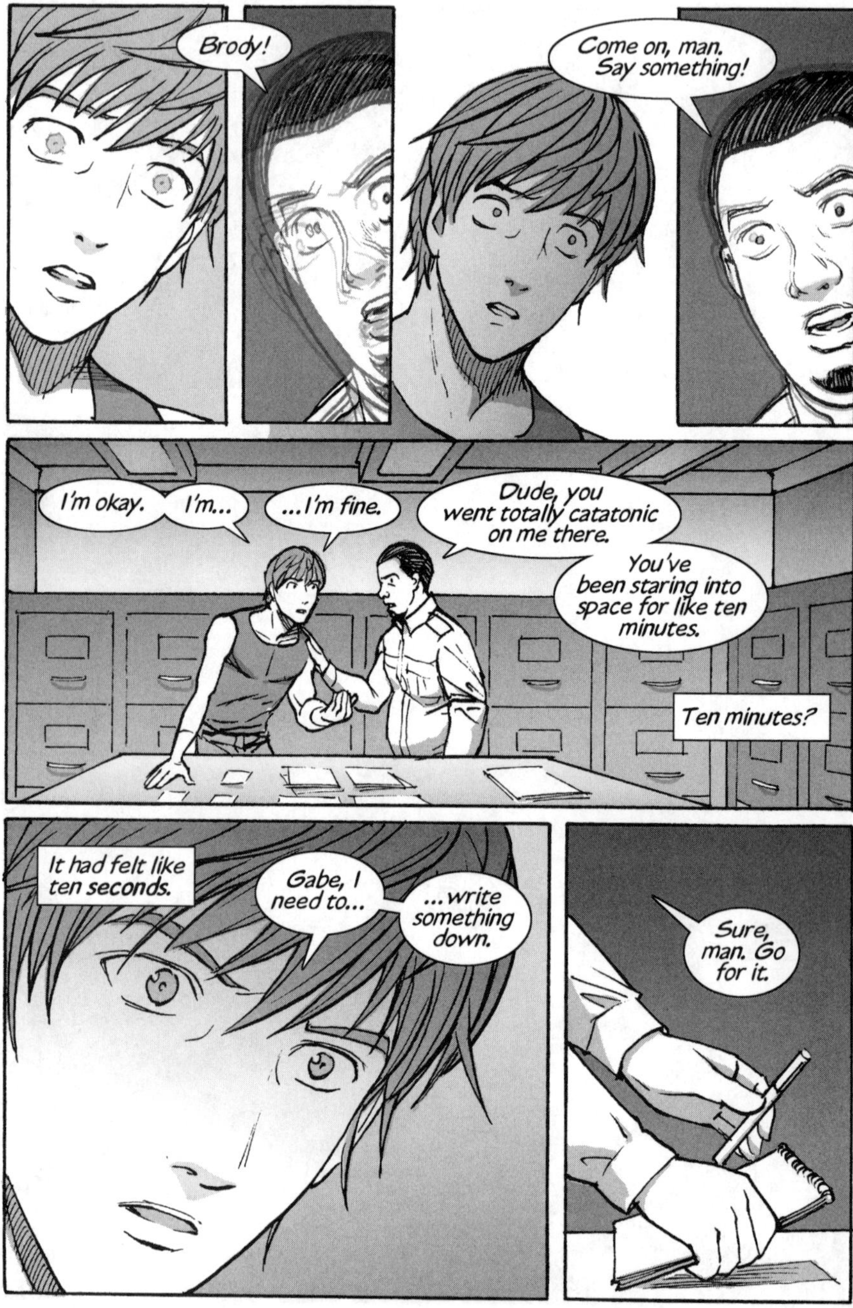
Brody!
Come on, man. Say something!
I'm okay.
I'm...
...I'm fine.
Dude, you went totally catatonic on me there.
You've been staring into space for like ten minutes.
Ten minutes?
It had felt like ten seconds.
Gabe, I need to...
...write something down.
Sure, man. Go for it.

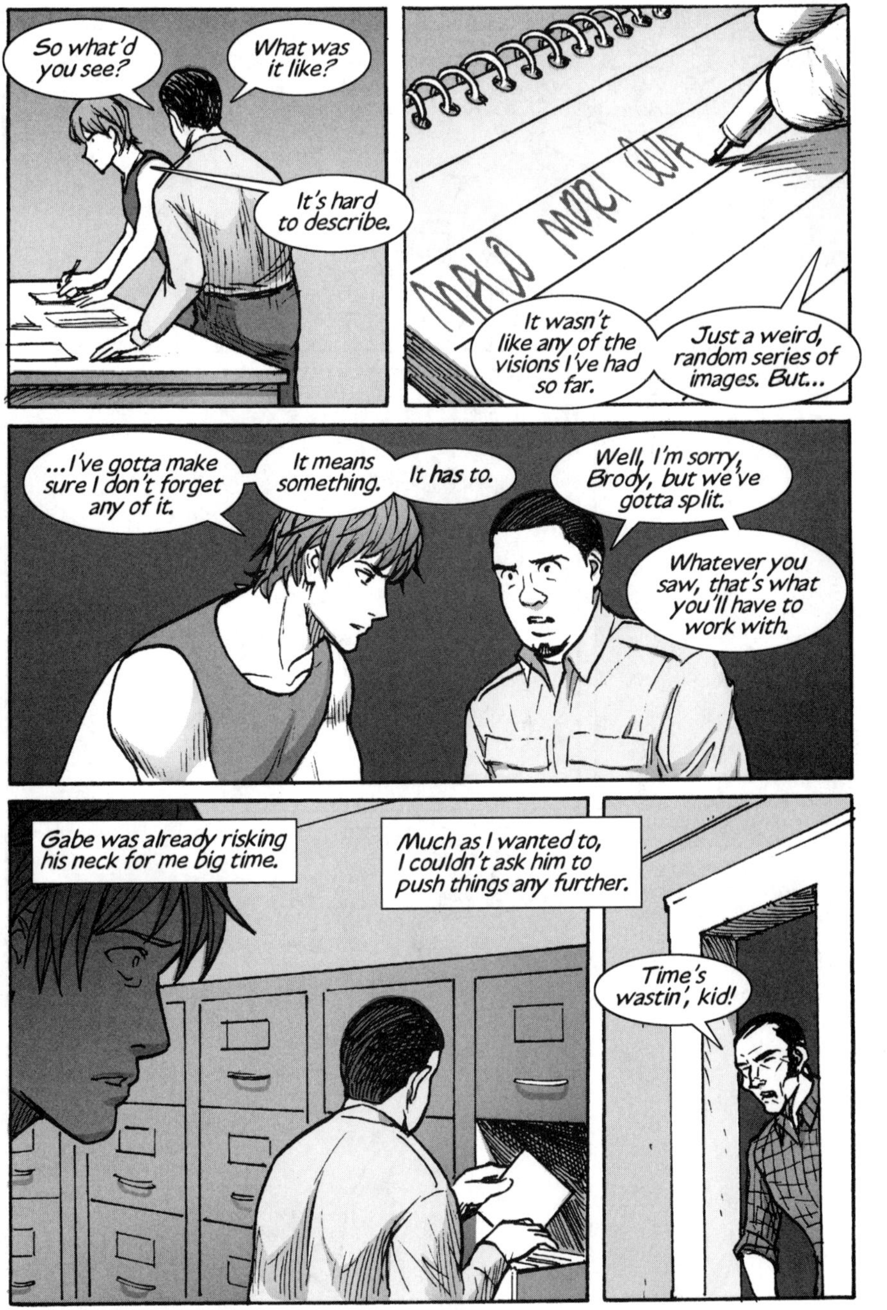

So what'd you see?
What was it like?
It's hard to describe.
MALO MORI QUA
It wasn't like any of the visions I've had so far.
Just a weird, random series of images. But...
...I've gotta make sure I don't forget any of it.
It means something.
It has to.
Well, I'm sorry, Brody, but we've gotta split.
Whatever you saw, that's what you'll have to work with.
Gabe was already risking his neck for me big time.
Much as I wanted to, I couldn't ask him to push things any further.
Time's wastin', kid!

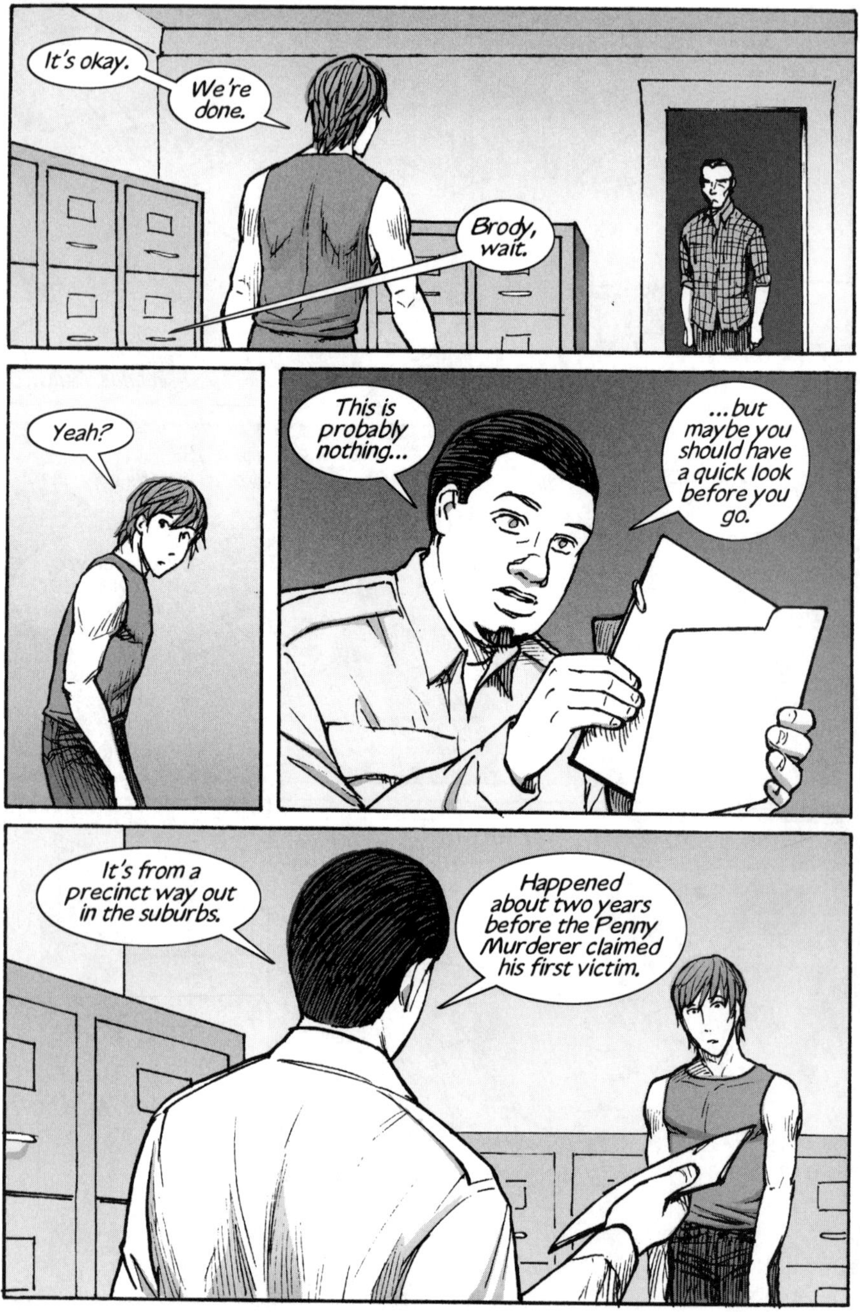
It's okay.
We're done.
Brody, wait.
Yeah?
This is probably nothing...
...but maybe you should have a quick look before you go.
It's from a precinct way out in the suburbs.
Happened about two years before the Penny Murderer claimed his first victim.

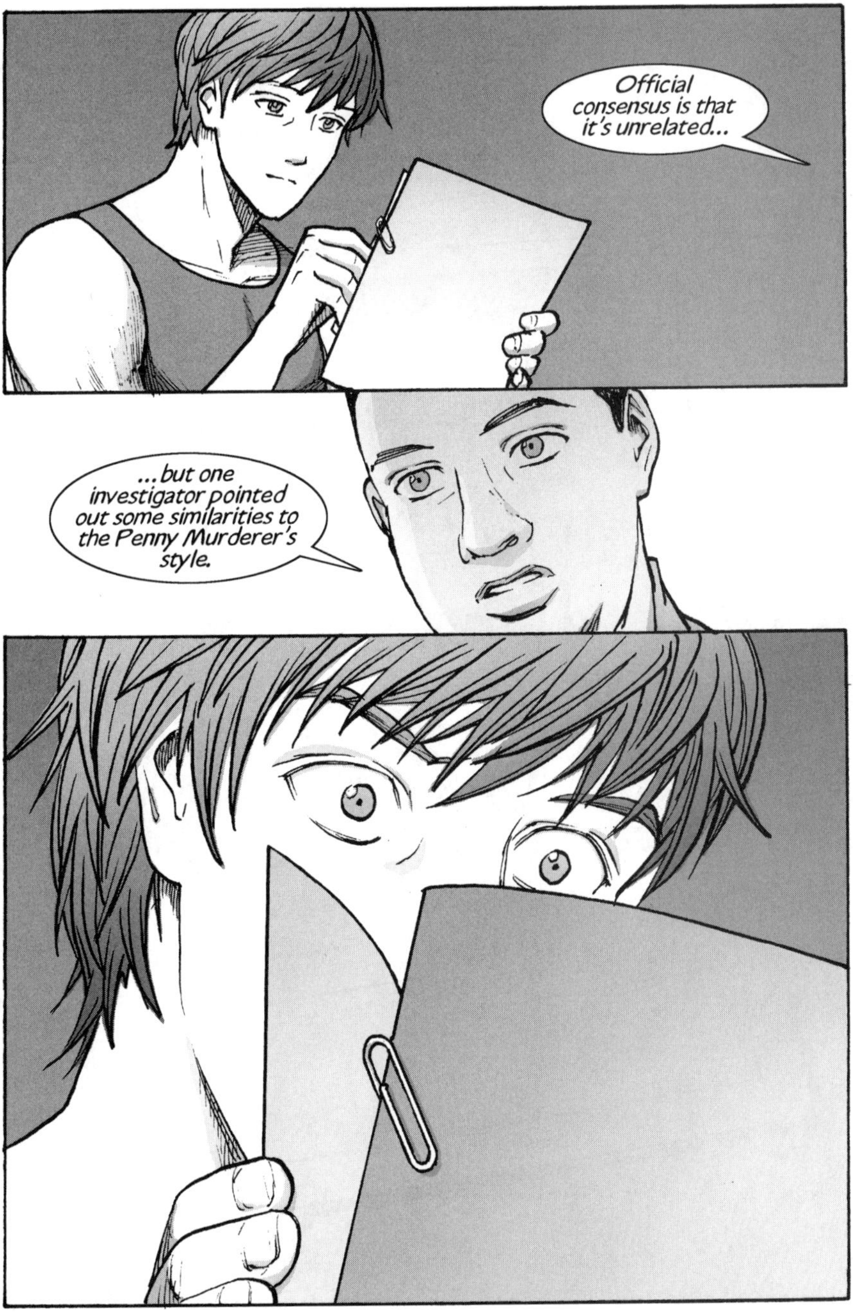
Official consensus is that it's unrelated...
...but one investigator pointed out some similarities to the Penny Murderer's style.

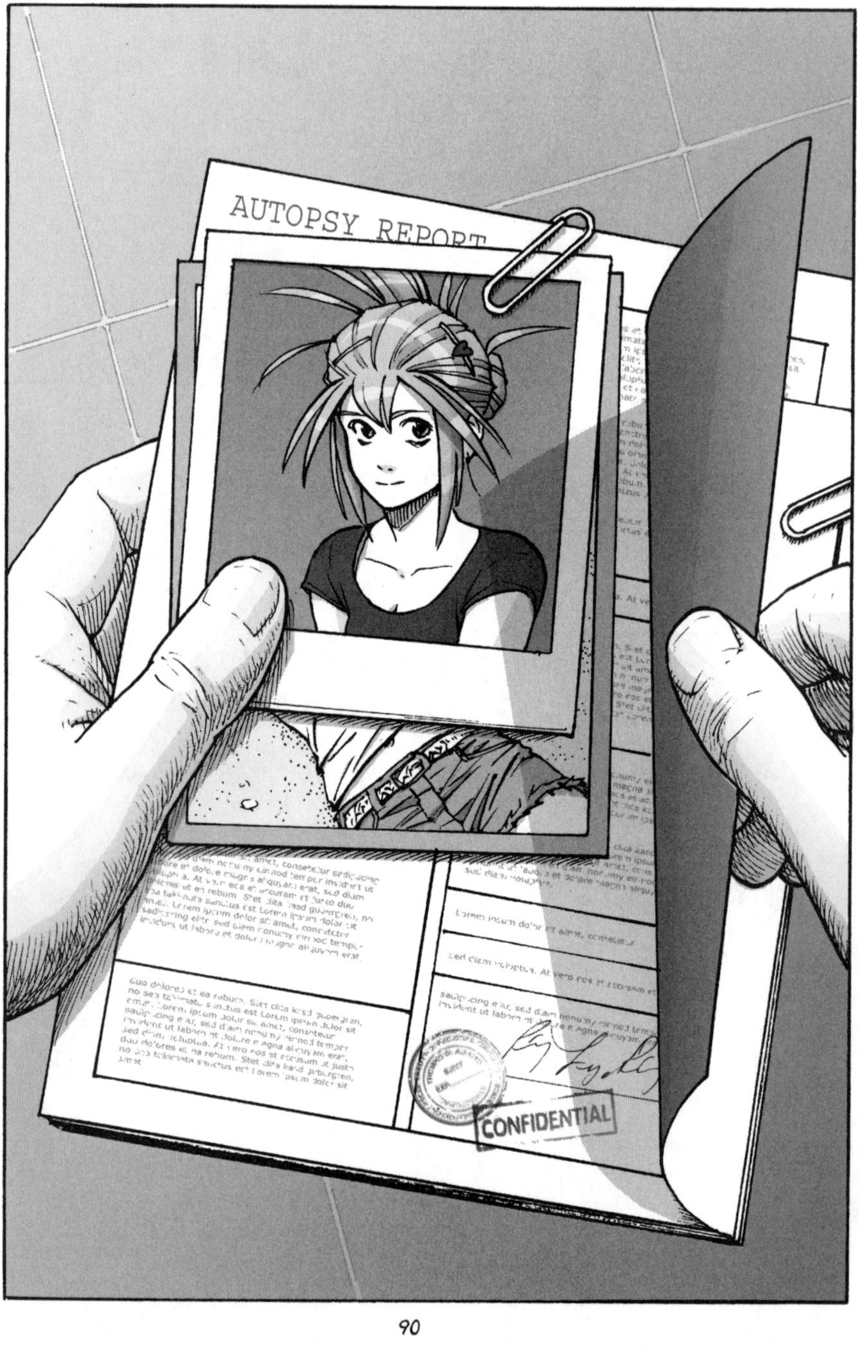
AUTOPSY REPORT
CONFIDENTIAL

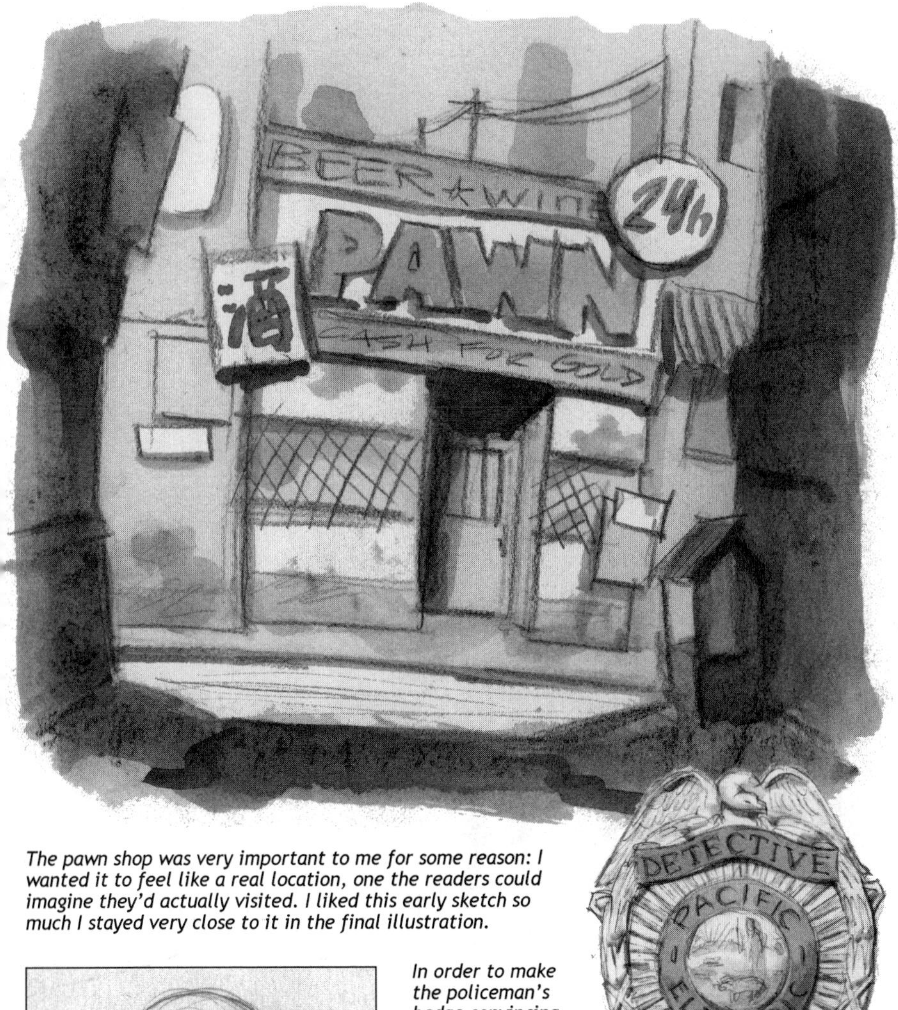
BEER☆WIN
24h
PAWN
酒
CASH FOR GOLD

The pawn shop was very important to me for some reason: I wanted it to feel like a real location, one the readers could imagine they'd actually visited. I liked this early sketch so much I stayed very close to it in the final illustration.

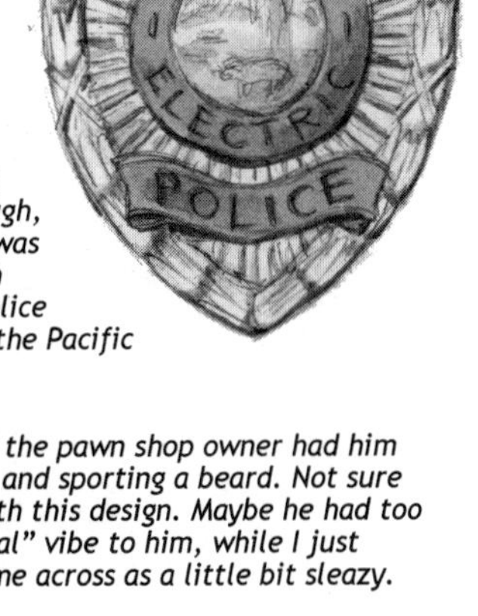
DETECTIVE
PACIFIC
ELECTRIC
POLICE

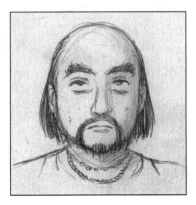

In order to make the policeman's badge convincing I based it on a photo of an actual badge. Oddly enough, the design I liked was from an early 20th century private police force working for the Pacific Electric Railway.

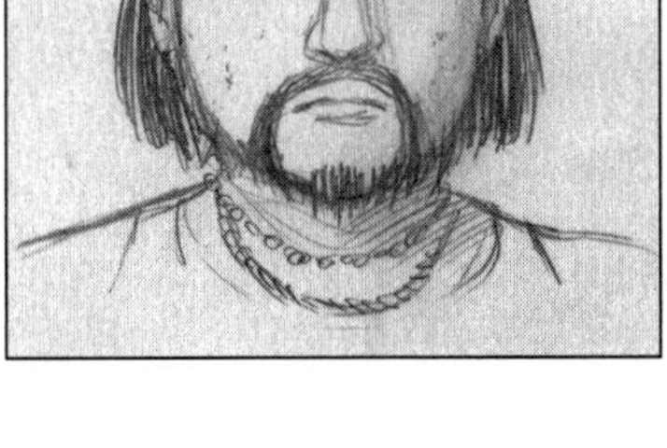

An early sketch of the pawn shop owner had him bald, long haired, and sporting a beard. Not sure why I didn't go with this design. Maybe he had too much of a "criminal" vibe to him, while I just wanted him to come across as a little bit sleazy.

The first sketch of the "heading to the coast" splash page showed the locale from a lower angle. I switched it to a bird's eye view to give it a bit more drama.

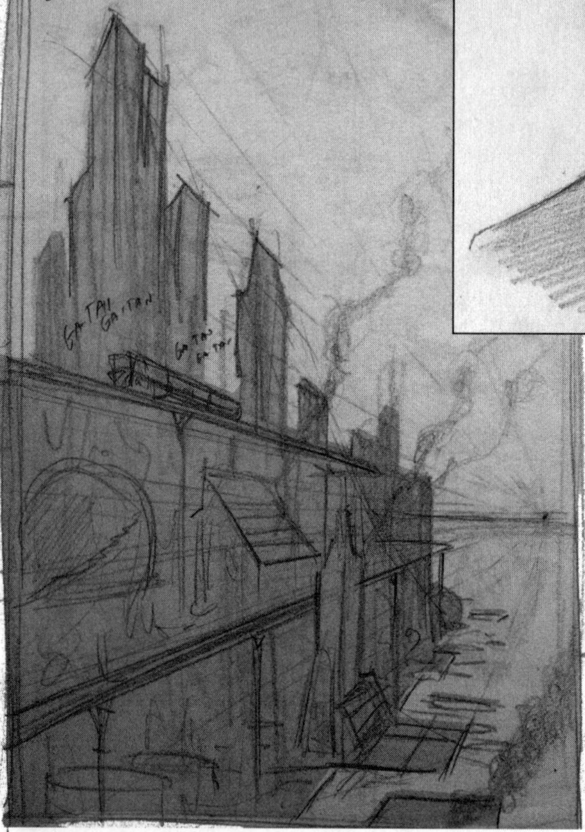

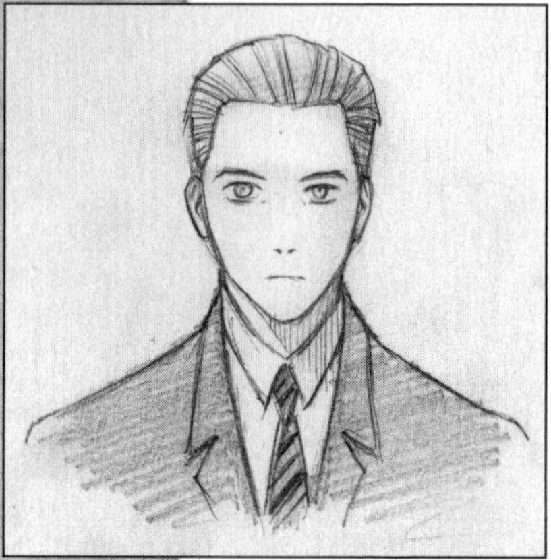

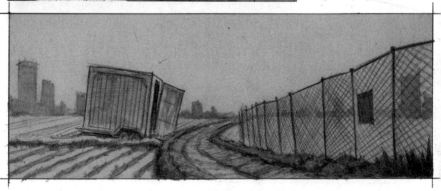

Early on I thought Brody might slick his hair back to play the part of Detective Jablonski. Giving it further thought, I decided many of the jokes would play better if he looked a little less cool and a little more geeky.

For the Sandra Hughes jogging sequence I knew I needed a place for the Penny Murderer to hide. At first I imagined an abandoned truck but there was something menacing about this image that gave away too much.Searching for alternatives, I settled on concrete segments from some sort of unfinished irrigation project.

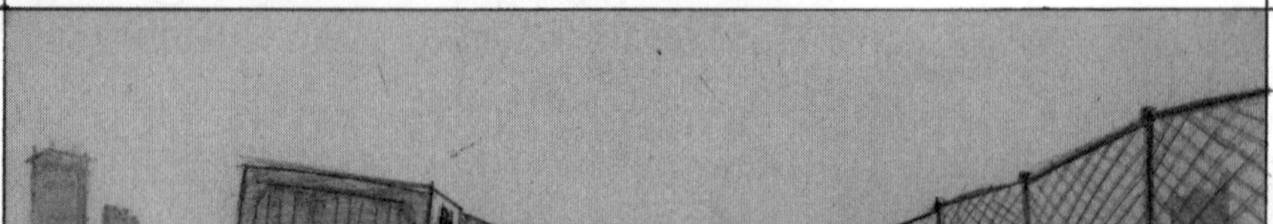

The establiching shot of the civic center involved teaching myself how to do lettering in an authentic "graffiti script."

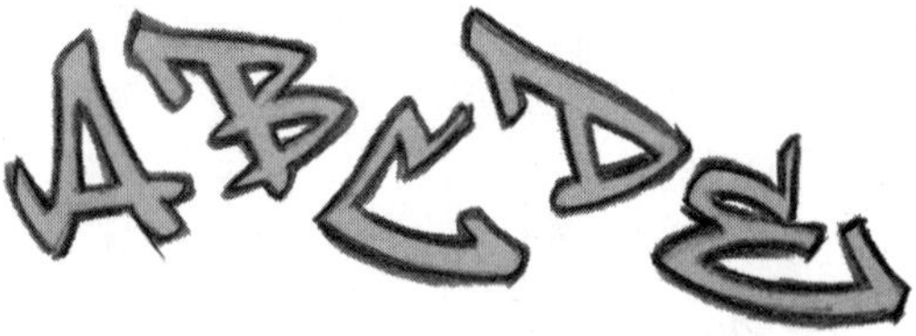
ABCDE

An early idea for Brody's method of getting into police headquarters was rather more humble: Two large boxes on a dolly. Very glad I changed this!

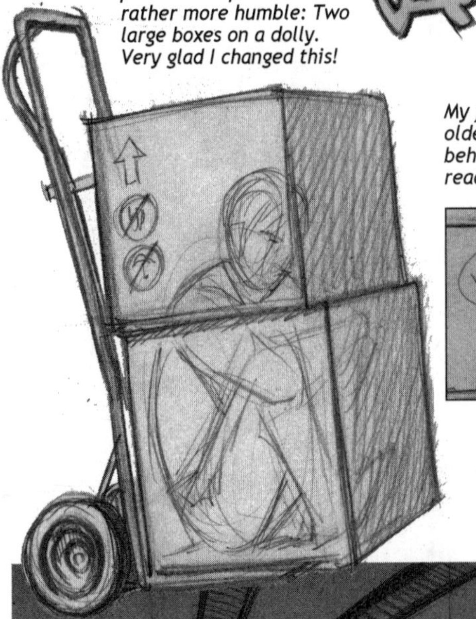

My first sketches of Splat had him considerably older and a little wall-eyed. As for the story behind his name, there is none! I wanted each reader to imagine his or her own explanation.

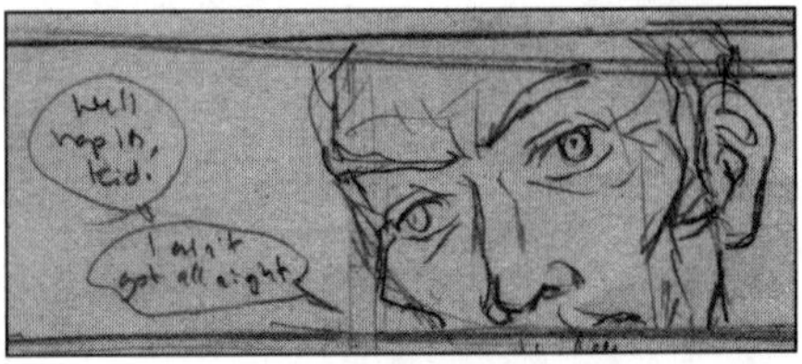
Well hop in, kid!
I ain't got all night

I knew I needed something pretty big and impressive for the civic center design. Some elements from this early sketch made it into the final version, but much of it just felt too cluttered to me.

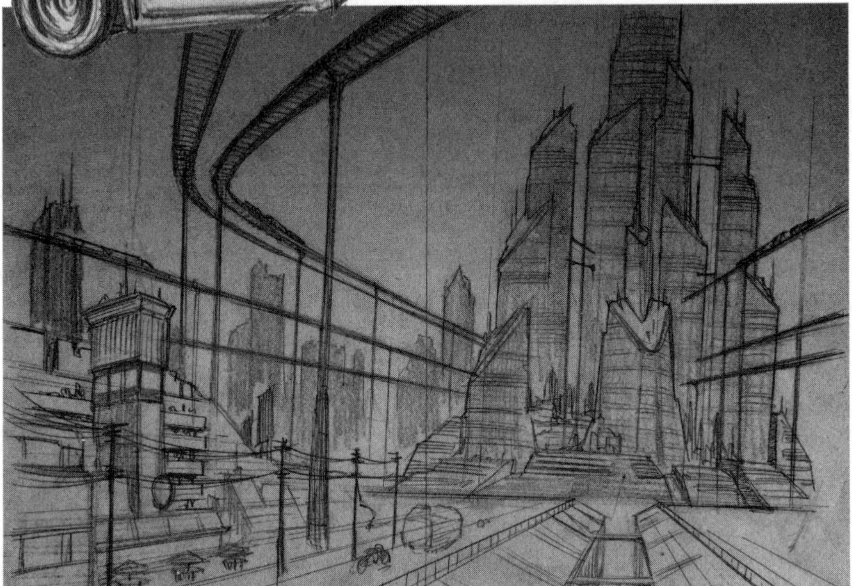

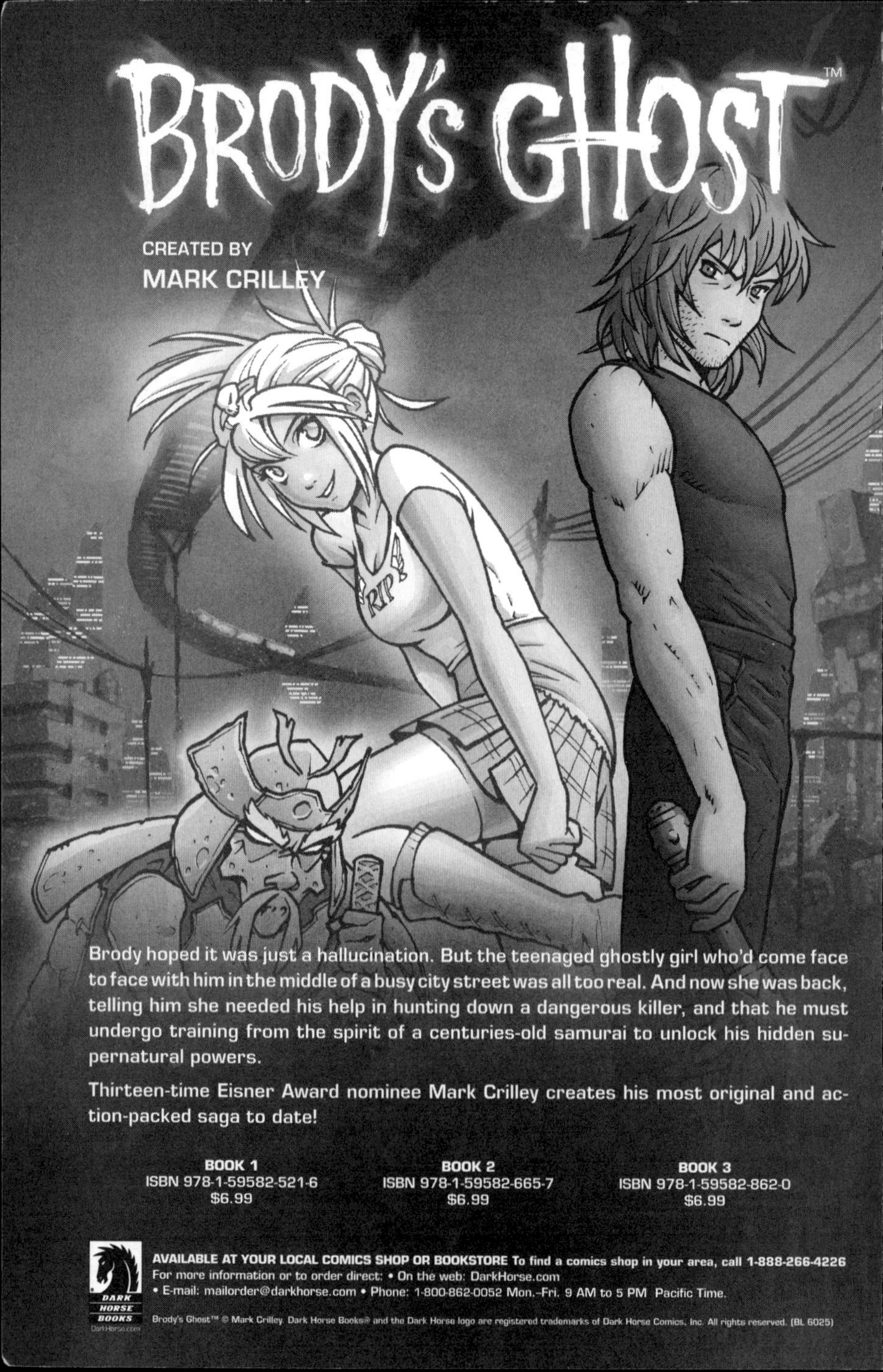
BRODY'S GHOST™
CREATED BY
MARK CRILLEY
RIP

Brody hoped it was just a hallucination. But the teenaged ghostly girl who'd come face to face with him in the middle of a busy city street was all too real. And now she was back, telling him she needed his help in hunting down a dangerous killer, and that he must undergo training from the spirit of a centuries-old samurai to unlock his hidden supernatural powers.

Thirteen-time Eisner Award nominee Mark Crilley creates his most original and action-packed saga to date!

BOOK 1
ISBN 978-1-59582-521-6
$6.99

BOOK 2
ISBN 978-1-59582-665-7
$6.99

BOOK 3
ISBN 978-1-59582-862-0
$6.99

DARK HORSE BOOKS
DarkHorse.com

AVAILABLE AT YOUR LOCAL COMICS SHOP OR BOOKSTORE To find a comics shop in your area, call **1-888-266-4226**
For more information or to order direct: • On the web: DarkHorse.com
• E-mail: mailorder@darkhorse.com • Phone: 1-800-862-0052 Mon.–Fri. 9 AM to 5 PM Pacific Time.

translucent

Can you see right through her?

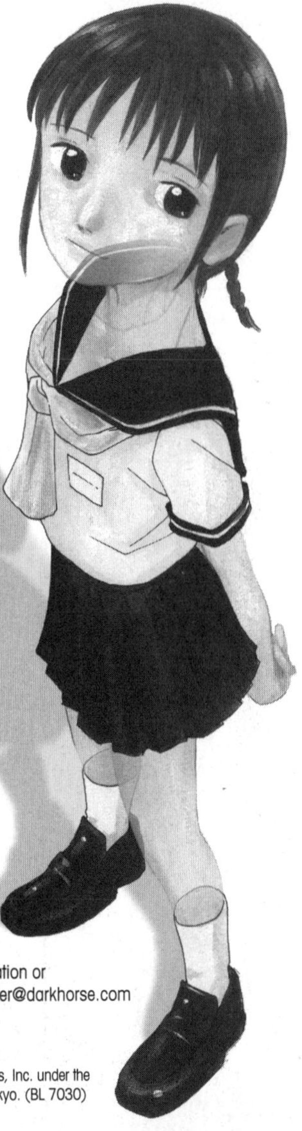

By Kazuhiro Okamoto

Shizuka is an introverted girl dealing with schoolwork, boys, and a medical condition that has begun to turn her invisible! She finds support with Mamoru, a boy who is falling for Shizuka despite her condition, and with Keiko, a woman who suffers from the same illness and has finally turned *completely* invisible! *Translucent's* exploration of what people see, what people think they see, and what people wish to see in themselves and others, makes for an emotionally sensitive manga peppered with moments of surprising humor, heartbreak, and drama.

VOLUME 1
ISBN 978-1-59307-647-4

VOLUME 2
ISBN 978-1-59307-677-1

VOLUME 3
ISBN 978-1-59307-679-5

$9.99 Each!

Previews for *TRANSLUCENT* and other DARK HORSE MANGA titles can be found at DarkHorse.com!

AVAILABLE AT YOUR LOCAL COMICS SHOP OR BOOKSTORE

To find a comics shop in your area, call 1-888-266-4226. For more information or to order direct: • On the web: DarkHorse.com • E-mail: mailorder@darkhorse.com • Phone: 1-800-862-0052 Mon.–Fri. 9 AM to 5 PM Pacific Time.

DARK HORSE MANGA

TRANSLUCENT © by Kazuhiro Okamoto. First published in Japan in 2005 by MEDIA FACTORY, Inc. English translation rights reserved by Dark Horse Comics, Inc. under the license from MEDIA FACTORY, Inc., Tokyo, through TOHAN CORPORATION, Tokyo. (BL 7030)

FINDER™

CARLA SPEED McNEIL

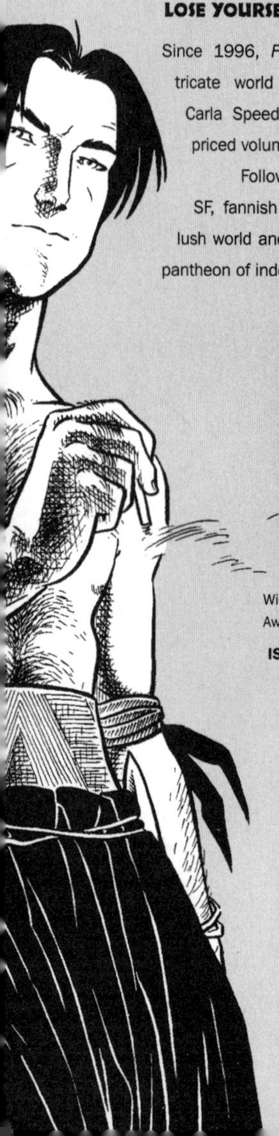

LOSE YOURSELF IN A WORLD BEYOND YOUR WILDEST DREAMS . . .

Since 1996, *Finder* has set the bar for science-fiction storytelling, with a lush, intricate world and compelling characters. Now, Dark Horse is proud to present Carla Speed McNeil's groundbreaking series in newly revised, expanded, affordably priced volumes!

Follow enigmatic hero Jaeger through a "glorious, catholic pileup of high-tech SF, fannish fantasy, and street-level culture clash" (*Village Voice*), and discover the lush world and compelling characters that have carved *Finder* a permanent place in the pantheon of independent comics.

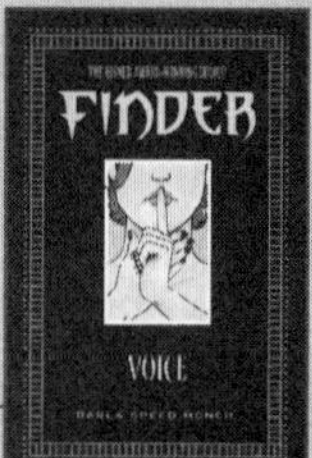
FINDER
VOICE
CARLA SPEED MCNEIL

FINDER: VOICE

Winner of the 2009 Eisner Award for Best Webcomic.

ISBN 978-1-59582-651-0

$19.99

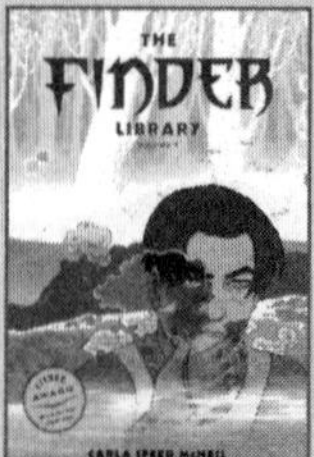
THE
FINDER
LIBRARY
CARLA SPEED McNEIL

THE FINDER LIBRARY VOLUME 1

Collecting the multiple Eisner Award-nominated story arcs "Sin Eater," "King of the Cats," and fan favorite "Talisman."

ISBN 978-1-59582-652-7

$24.99

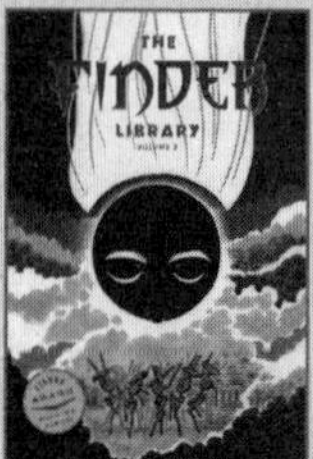
THE
FINDER
LIBRARY
CARLA SPEED McNEIL

THE FINDER LIBRARY VOLUME 2

Collecting "Dream Sequence," "Mystery Date," "The Rescuers," and "Five Crazy Women."

ISBN 978-1-59582-653-4

$24.99

To find a comics shop in your area, call 1-888-266-4226
For more information or to order direct: On the web: DarkHorse.com
E-mail: mailorder@darkhorse.com
Phone: 1-800-862-0052
Mon–Fri 9 AM to 5 PM Pacific Time

DARK HORSE COMICS®
DarkHorse.com